IT'S HARD
TO FIGHT
naked

IT'S HARD TO FIGHT
naked

NIECY NASH

GALLERY BOOKS

New York   London   Toronto   Sydney   New Delhi

Gallery Books
A Division of Simon & Schuster, Inc.
1230 Avenue of the Americas
New York, NY 10020

First Gallery Books hardcover edition April 2013

GALLERY BOOKS and colophon are registered trademarks of Simon & Schuster, Inc.

For information about special discounts for bulk purchases, please contact Simon & Schuster Special Sales at 1-866-506-1949 or business@ simonandschuster.com.

The Simon & Schuster Speakers Bureau can bring authors to your live event. For more information or to book an event contact the Simon & Schuster Speakers Bureau at 1-866-248-3049 or visit our website at www .simonspeakers.com.

Designed by Jaime Putorti

Manufactured in the United States of America

10 9 8 7 6 5 4 3 2 1

Library of Congress Cataloging-in-Publication Data

Nash, Niecy
    It's hard to fight naked / Niecy Nash. — First Gallery Books hardcover edition.
        p. cm
1. Dating (Social customs) 2. Man-woman relationships. 3. Interpersonal relations. I. Title.
    HQ801.N37 2013
    306.73—dc23   2012044537

ISBN 978-1-4516-8772-9
ISBN 978-1-4516-8774-3 (ebook)

I dedicate this book to my husband, Jay Tucker.

You are the confirmation of the things I've believed all my life: That love is patient and kind, that there are men who want to be faithful, that relationships can be easy with the right partner, and that second chances are sometimes better than the first. You are my best friend, my confidant, my favorite lover. Thank you for being the very sexy answer to a heartfelt prayer. With you I've learned so many things about relationships, including the fact that it's hard to fight naked. If we ever have to fight, I'm always happy to be naked with you. . . .

With all my love and good stuff,

Niecy Nash

IT'S HARD
TO FIGHT
naked

introduction

Let's get one thing out of the way right quick: I am *not* a hopeless romantic—people have called me that my whole life and it has never made any sense to me. What's hopeless about being a romantic? How can you even *be* both? What I am is a girl who is in love with LOVE!

I can't explain why. I don't ever remember feeling any different. When I was a little girl, they called me boy crazy. My mother used to say I had a "touchy-feely gene." I was in kindergarten when I decided that a boy named Robert was going to be my boyfriend. I'm not sure how I knew at such a young age that boys were visual creatures, but I knew. So one day I begged my grandma to let me wear my purple velvet dress, white kneesocks, black patent-leather shoes, and . . . wait for it . . . a rabbit-fur jacket! I wanted Robert to see me in my kindergarten finest.

I also learned early on from observing my parents that a guy is happy when he's well fed, so when I offered Robert that Now and Later candy I had hidden in my sock, I sealed the deal! I tried to hold his hand, too, which he thought was weird, but I didn't care. If he was gonna eat my candy, he was gonna have to hold my hand—even as a five-year-old I could have told him that! It was all so innocent, and it was just the beginning of my journey with this thing called love.

I've been a wife and an ex-wife, and I'm a child of divorce, but I've always firmly believed that we were put on this earth to find love. And there ain't nothing hopeless about that! I believed it even when things didn't go right for me, when I was wailing and gnashing my teeth on the floor with a knife in my heart and my girlfriends were screaming, "There ain't no good men left!" Every time that happened (and there were many times!) I always thought, *The next time I fall in love it's gonna be different!* Holla if you hear me. . . .

When I divorced my first husband, nobody thought that was strange—all anyone said was "Girl, join the club!" To my surprise, the real record scratch was when I told people I'd found love again. "Say *what* now?!" That was when I realized that too many people had given up on love, whether or not they'd ever experienced it in the first place.

Hell, yes, I found love, and you need to find it, too! Society has played a horrible trick on us, duped us into believing that we can go it alone, that we can do bad all by ourselves—that when the going gets tough, we gotta go at it alone. I've always refused to accept that! We're all supposed to have a partner in crime. Why? Because someone has to drive the getaway car!

Labor Day 2009, I approached Jay Tucker on a dance floor (while he was dancing with another woman!), and twelve months later to the day he put a ring on it—this after I'd had a divorce under my belt and three kids in tow. Now, I love that man more than anything else, but he's not the reason I'm writing this book. This isn't some "I got my man, where's yours?" kind of thing. Just to be clear, I'm not a self-proclaimed expert on love. But I have been through some things and often share my experiences with women and men alike in an effort to make love easier—literally and figuratively. I want to start a dialogue outside of traditional norms and introduce a new way of creating, experiencing, and enjoying the relationship we deserve. I also want to dispel the myth that men are the complicated ones—sorry, ladies! We've got way more going on than they do. Just keep reading. I promise we will have fun navigating this thing we call LOVE.

A few months after Jay and I started dating, we decided to throw a matchmaker party at our house for all the single folks we knew in Los Angeles. And it was a *huge* success—just ask *The View*'s Sherri Shepherd. She met the man she'd eventually marry right in my kitchen! Word spread across Hollywood like a pregnancy rumor, and now I can't accommodate half the women trying to get in. And it's not just because I like to keep a clean house! Unfortunately it's because most women come to me with an attitude something like this:

"Girl, I'm sick of the lies, I'm sick of men, I'm sick of it all. My ex was crazy and I'm just *tired*. I just give and give, and they treat me worse than someone off the street. But if you have another matchmaker party, I definitely want to be there!"

Hell, no, her ass ain't coming to any matchmaker party of mine. With an attitude like that, she's already chosen her own adventure of unhappiness. But even though this attitude won't get you a party invite, I'd hate to leave anyone suffering alone in the dark. So whether you're looking to find love for the first time, in need of renewed faith after a heartbreak, or trying to keep what you've got from dying on the vine, I want to help everyone discover the best possible relationship. For some of you that will require a considerable amount of work. You've got to become whole, you've got to forgive your ex to be ready for your next, and you've got to be willing to be vulnerable. I know—it's a big thing I'm asking you to do, right? But once you take the right steps toward getting the love you deserve, the returns will come in sooner than you might expect. And if it takes my serving you up a tall glass of act-right first to get there, so be it. *That's* why I decided to write this book.

Originally, I wanted to call it *Stomach Full, Penis Empty: A Woman's Guide to a Happy Marriage* but that would have been a pretty short book. Plus, Walmart probably wouldn't shelve it with a title like that, and this is a message that everyone—single or in a relationship—needs to hear. Dating and relationships can be profoundly simple once we strip away years of misinformation and learn how to communicate honestly with one another. Men speak in headlines and women speak in fine print, but that doesn't mean we aren't trying to write the same story.

Now, as "touchy-feely" as Mother says I may be, no one ever comes to me for advice expecting me to give it to 'em easy. So when you need it straight up with no chaser, I'll be the first one to serve it to you. We're going to tackle some tough subjects, but I'm not giving you a list of rules to follow, and I'm not always going to tell you what you want to hear.

But experience is a good teacher, and I've spent *way* too many years recording history in beauty salons, spas, bathrooms, and everywhere else in between where women get to talking about relationships and dating. I've heard every last piece of traditional advice on whom to give up it to, how to give it up, and when to just give up altogether—and I invite you to leave all of that behind if it hasn't worked for you. Some of what I've learned won't be popular with your girlfriends. (I scratch my weave when women give each other arbitrary rules to follow and outline elaborate plans as if this were some big game we're playing and men were these wildly complex beasts we have to come up against. Trust me— they're not!)

Allow me to simplify this for you *and* for men: The whole thing comes down to honesty, first with yourself, and then with them. So, if you are ready to walk in your truth, I'm here to take the sting out of this whole love thing—whether it's finding it, keeping it, knowing when to let go of it, or readying yourself to find it again. I invite you to leave your negativity at the door and begin to think differently.

I want it to be easy for you to be honest with yourself and others. I want it to be easy for you to communicate what you want and trust that your partner will give it to you. I also want you to discover how hard it is to fight naked. The greatest gifts and blessings you give and receive come from a state when we're at our most vulnerable. So come on, y'all—let's get naked!

chapter one

WANTING TO BE READY FOR LOVE DOESN'T MAKE IT SO

That you're reading this book tells me you've come to a point in your life where you're eager to find love, to feel love, and to share love with another person. And as simple as love should be, simply wanting all these things is not enough. That's not to say that love isn't waiting around the corner for you; it just means that it may take a little bit of prep work, *because a goal without a plan is just a wish*. And I should know—it wasn't very long ago that I had to do it all myself.

After my first marriage ended, I didn't wait long to throw myself back into the deep end of the dating pool, and pretty quickly I met a man I'll never forget. He wasn't my next husband, but he did a damn good job of getting me on the path to finding him. This man and I had been hanging out with for a few months, and naturally I started thinking

I was back on track, so I said something to him like "You and me, we've really got something here," and that's when he hit me back with something I never expected to hear.

"I appreciate the fact that you're interested in me," he said tenderly. "But I would much rather date you when you're whole."

Uhh, excuse me? What are you trying to say? I let him explain himself as tears welled up in my eyes.

"It's like you're a runner in a race. I would much rather try to chase you when you're in the best shape of your life, to be alongside you at the Olympics. But right now, I feel like I'm running after that white woman with a broken leg in a scary movie."

Well, I crumbled. Not because he told me what I didn't want to hear, but because what he said was true. It was up to me to recognize it and own that I was a broken bag of bones. He saw that I was coming at this whole thing from a fragile place. Not only did he not want to take advantage of me, he also realized that starting a relationship with someone who wasn't ready to be in one wouldn't do him any good either.

Eventually, I came to appreciate his compassion *and* his discernment—I only wished I'd had the wisdom to pick up on it myself. But that I was finally able to see myself clearly meant that the healing had begun. Because, you see, *you need to be whole before you give up the hole*. I know that sounds raw, but sometimes you just need to hear it that way. The decision to share your body with a man includes sharing your soul, so you have to be strategic about the "soul ties" you create. Unfortunately, the world is not full of caring men as eager to help you find your way, which is how you find yourself lying up with someone who's dropping you off at work in *your* car, playing video games, and eating cereal in his underwear all day. Hello?! You cannot trust the decisions you make when you are broken!

The universe is going to send you somebody great, but why would it ever send the best for you when you're not at your best? Sadly, it comes down to this: wanting to be in a relationship and being equipped for one are two different things, and being ready to receive requires a certain level of preparedness. Before you head out into the great unknown, a few key things must be addressed so that you are fully prepared.

IF YOU FEEL THAT THERE ARE NO GOOD MEN LEFT, KEEP YOUR ASS AT HOME

Hopefully that doesn't sound to harsh right off the bat! I'd hate to lose you before we even got started on the important work. But sometimes I feel that I need to shake people out of stinkin' thinkin'. It's easy to get into a rut, and it's totally reasonable for any of us to find ourselves in one. I just hate to see anyone stuck, though, when I honestly believe that love is out there waiting for you—but your eyes and heart *have* to be open to it, which I hope this chapter is able to help you do. From here on out, we're in this together.

Not too long ago, I was at a Super Bowl party jam-packed with celebrity after celebrity. Everyone was excited to be there for one reason or another until a woman so toxic that her stink eye cleared a path wherever she walked, leaving men running away in her wake. With her ill-fitting outfit and her mouth twisted to the side, everyone clearly knew that she'd been suffering for a while (which is a nice way of saying she'd been celibate, and not by choice!). So there she was, offending everybody at the bar, saying things like "He was only pretending to be interested in you" and "This party is full of dogs. Why did we even come?" Before long, each of her friends left, and they all left alone. Had she brought her nonsense my way, I would have told her the same thing I tell any woman who feels unlucky in love. I can't stay at your pity party long, but I do invite you to take responsibility for your unhappiness and recognize that it is something you can control. Because, yes, you have the right to be upset and feel hurt and dismayed by love when you've been wronged, and I don't want to rob you of that time to grieve, but I want you to realize that the power to change your destiny belongs to you. Once you're ready to take charge of it all, once you've determined you have the wherewithal to move on from the pain of your past, the power lies within you.

Before you get into any relationship, the person who you really have to know is yourself. Being mad at the world, living in a perpetual state of suffering, accepting things that are not edifying you—all of this has to die so that you can live fully. When you're able to identify and overcome the circumstances of your past that are keeping you down, when you put out God's best version of you into the world, you will then attract what you are—a whole, healthy human *becoming*. (I don't like the word *being* because it suggests a state of permanence, and I like to think we're always evolving.)

If I'm not making myself clear, let me tell it to you straight (without elaborating too much, for the sake of my mother and my babies, on the details of my love life!). The last time I didn't have a frank enough discussion with myself about what I wanted out of life, within months I went from being married to a preacher in the Valley to dating the number one stripper in East Orange, New Jersey. Now I don't have anything against strippers, but if I had been honest with myself, I would have been able to see that although he was a great guy, we did not want the same thing. Instead I wasted a whole year trying to put a square peg in a round hole! I wanted to feel protected, and I wanted to feel validated, but I didn't ask myself anything beyond that. And when I failed to pull together an accurate description of what I wanted out of a man, I got a whole lotta applicants to be my boyfriend who weren't the right person for the job.

Remember that love is patient and love is kind, and it is all those other things you hear people reciting at their weddings. But you have to love yourself first. If you believe that God or the universe is going to send you somebody great, why would he ever be sent when you aren't ready to receive? No man will love you more than you love yourself, and you need to feel valuable, to understand what you're bringing to the party, and trust that *you're going to attract what you are*. Once you get there, you're well on your way to finding a good thing.

WHEN YOU ARE HONEST ABOUT WHAT YOU WANT, YOU'RE MORE LIKELY TO GET IT

I don't know how many times I've heard a woman say, "I'm sure I'll eventually get married, but I'm in no rush." And then every Sunday her boyfriend is trying to watch football and she's watching *Say Yes to the Dress* or stopping in her tracks each time she walks past a jewelry store, yet she tells her man that she's not in any rush to get serious. Double-mindedness like that is sure to get any woman in trouble. There is no sense in pretending to be what you think a man wants from you. Are you looking for companionship? Do you want a husband? Or are you just looking for somebody to hang out with? You have to know the answers to these questions before you get out there, so that you can start asking for what you want!

When I met Jay, in the first five minutes he asked me if I wanted to have kids. I wasn't sure which answer he wanted, but rather than lie, I said, "I got my tubes tied, cut, and burned. I can't give you anything but a good time."

He looked at me as if he'd heard angels singing. "Do you want to get married?"

"Hell, yeah," I said without hesitating. "I did it once and was married for sixteen years, and I would do it again in a heartbeat for the right man."

When I asked Jay later what he thought of our first conversation, he told me that he didn't want any children and he was looking for a wife. If I didn't want to get married or if I was looking to have kids, he said there would have been no reason to take it any further.

I think a lot of people might hesitate before answering where they fall on the marriage-kids spectrum, not wanting to say the wrong thing and potentially squander a promising opportunity for a relationship. How promising can an opportunity be when you don't want the same thing? But that is precisely the problem with keeping up appearances rather than owning up to what you want for yourself from the universe and not settling for anything less. That's the only way you're going to find the right man for you—it starts with finding someone who shares

THERE'S NOTHING CUTE ABOUT A "FRENEMY"

Just because someone is an old friend doesn't mean she can't be your biggest enemy when it comes to finding love. Here are some surefire ways to spot ultimately unsupportive sisters.

- ▶ When you phone her to say someone broke your heart, she calls you right back. But when she knows you've met someone cute, you won't hear from her all week.

- ▶ She always knows what you've been doing "wrong," but rarely has any bright ideas on how you might do anything "right."

- ▶ She always finds something wrong with the guy you're dating and never recognizes what you might see in him.

- ▶ Her compliments usually boost her up more than they do you.

your vision for the future. It's not about having the *right* answer; it's about knowing what you want. It's just as easy to love a man who wants what you want as it is to love one who doesn't!

Now, I'm not telling you that you need to bang out this conversation in the first five minutes the way Jay and I did—to be honest, that would probably scare away most men . . . and women, for that matter. But I can tell you that *most* men don't lie about two things: whether they want to get married and whether they want to have kids. Believe when people tell you who they are the first time. They know themselves much better than you. They might lie when you ask if they've been arrested, or lie about the neighborhood they grew up in or the schools they went to, but when you ask a man if he's interested in a committed relationship, if he sees a family in his future, and he tells you no, he ain't lying. And sticking around to learn more about someone who doesn't want what you want is just a waste of your precious time.

OPEN YOURSELF UP
TO BEING HURT

$\mathcal{I}$’ve been hurt before—some would say I let my guard down prematurely—and I got the rug pulled right out from under me. For most people, once they’ve been hurt, they spend the rest of their lives trying to avoid ever feeling that way again. While I understand that urge, it’s just not how I operate—nor is it productive. Everyone would rather end up together than alone—it’s human nature. See, I would much rather have the possible temporary pain from opening myself to the chance of something greater, because I know I can handle disappointment. I’ve been there and done that, and it’s a sting that I know will eventually go away. My need for love, however, never fades. It's why acting in service of love instead of giving in to fear should be easy breezy, potta-peasy.

Now, I know it sounds foolish, but here's my theory: you cannot love fully—emphasis on *fully*—without being vulnerable, without risking whatever it "all" is to you. Is being completely in control more important than letting go of some less healthy behaviors? Is proving you can do this on your own more fulfilling than discovering a new part of yourself by being with someone else?

Sure, it gets tricky when you've been burned before, but here's where wisdom comes in. You can be so hurt in a relationship that you're devastated, crushed, and damaged. But successfully coming out on the other side of that pain isn't about saying, "I'm going to allow myself to love again, but I'm only going to let him get so close" or "I won't let myself be that open or damaged again." It's about recognizing that the next choice you make is yours; *you* get to decide what kind of a relationship you want to be in. And you have to trust that in the next go-round you'll be capable of making a decision based on what you've learned about yourself and your past relationships.

I believe that most people don't walk into a relationship with the malicious intent to hurt another person. It's just that we all want all the blessings of love, without ever doing anything to test it, and that's simply not how it works. When you order a number one at McDonald's, you don't open the bag when you get home and say, "Who the hell put these fries in here?" Fries come with the burger every time. Unfortunately with love, you're always going to get pain—which is a raw deal compared to a tasty bag of salty, fried goodness, but it's unavoidable. Just because you're in love doesn't mean that you're never again going to feel hurt or disappointed. It's just the opposite. But once you accept that love comes with pain and you have faith in your choice of mate—because you made that choice when you were whole—restoring a relationship to a better place and getting over any relationship grief is easier. You can get back to loving much more quickly when you recognize that the pain that you suffer in a relationship isn't a willful act on anyone's part. As soon as you settle on that, you'll be all right. Unfortunately we can't control what happens to us. We can only control how we respond.

When she says, "I'm not in a hurry to have kids"—
She means "I want to have kids."

When he says, "I'm not really interested in having kids"—
He means "I don't want kids."

When she says, "Pssh, all men are dogs"—
She means "How long do I have to hold out before
settling for a dog?"

When he says, "I'm not looking for something very serious"—
He means "I don't want a commitment
but I will have sex with you."

When she says, "I only date athletes"—
She means "I haven't figured out what's really
important to me yet."

PREFERENCES VERSUS PRIORITIES

$\mathcal{I}$'m sure you've seen Sherri Shepherd cutting up as cohost on *The View* and stealing scenes playing Tracy Morgan's wife on *30 Rock*. You also probably watched her bawl her eyes out when she was eliminated from *Dancing with the Stars*. (I was proud of us both for making it as far as we did in our respective seasons, but c'mon now, girl— neither of us was ever going to win with curves like ours!) Not long ago, Sherri felt just as rejected by the dating game, though what she didn't realize was that she had thrown *herself* out of the competition long before it even started—all because of a misguided set of criteria she'd invented.

Not long after Jay and I were engaged, we threw our first matchmaker party, and though Sherri was a little reluctant, I made sure she came by. Now Sherri is big on personality but short on stature (sound like anyone else you know?), and at five feet one inch she's always dated men on the shorter side of the spectrum. However, not thirty minutes after she showed up at the party, one of Jay's friends lumbered all six feet six inches of himself over to me and whispered, "Who is that little loud one over there? I want that one!" I told him to hold tight, because I already knew about Sherri's height hang-ups, and sure enough, when I pointed the gentle giant out to her, she panicked, hollering, "Oh, no, girl. He's way too big for me! You know I like little guys!"

By this time, Sherri had been divorced from her first husband for over a year and had a four-year-old boy at home. Before she had the chance to say anything more, I said, "No, Sherri. Let me correct you. I know you. What's ultimately going to make you happy is a man who can take your son to the doctor when he's sick and you have to work. A man who can cook because: number one, the Lord knows you can't, and number two, you need someone who can help you stay on top of your diabetes. No matter how tall, how small, how wide—all of that doesn't mean a damn if your needs aren't being met." Sherri had been letting her preferences—bite-size and gainfully employed—lead the charge, when she should have been trying to find a man who would meet her emotional needs and give her the support she deserved. I ran into the other room to grab Big Papa, and by the time we got back to the kitchen, Sherri had slipped out the front door!

Lucky for her, I knew where to find her, and the next day I called and convinced her to agree to a phone date. My objective was simple: to get Sherri to have a conversation with this man without all of her preferences getting in the way of determining whether he satisfied her priorities. I knew that if she could experience this guy for the kind and funny man that he was, she could make a real, lasting connection with him.

Cut to the next day: I'm watching *The View* and I see my girl draaagging up there. I called her right away and said, "What's got you all sleepy-eyed today? I only asked you to agree to a ten-minute phone date." Her answer? "We were on the phone for six hours last night!" That man was Lamar Sally, and eighteen months later, I was a bridesmaid in their wedding! So get into that!

Now I can't tell you what *your* priorities are—but I can tell you that they are the nonnegotiable things that have nothing to do with vanity. Make a checklist for yourself of the things you look for in a man, then organize them into priorities and preferences. That way you have a clearer picture of the man you want that has nothing to do with the superficial things you thought you wanted that get old fast.

When you date for your preferences, all you wind up with is a collection of people who all look the same and act the same, and all of them together aren't worth a damn! You could wrap 'em up and sell them for ten cents. It's when you start dating for your priorities that you find yourself in relationships that are full of contentment and emotional satisfaction.

NO ONE'S ASKING
YOU TO SETTLE!

*B*efore I judge Sherri too harshly, I should point out that *most* people mistake their preferences in men for their priorities. So let me make this simple: preferences are the things you look for in a hookup; priorities are the qualities you seek in a long-term mate. It doesn't take long to find the right guy when you're honest with yourself about what you want and you're only willing to accept what you need.

We've all been socialized to believe in happily ever after, to believe that we're each a princess awaiting a man to come in on a horse and take us back to his castle. We've been programmed to think that Malibu Barbie

and Ken had it going on. But I've gone on enough con-
vertible rides to recognize that when you put unrealistic expectations on people you meet, everyone ends up
disappointed. There's only one perfect man, and he was
hung up on a cross two thousand years ago—if your man
were perfect, that would mean you'd have to be, too, and
who has the time, patience, or energy for that? And who
can even achieve that? Even Martha Stewart ended up in
jail trying that one.

I'm not asking you to stick your hand in a bag full of
uglies and pull one out either—there's got to be something about your man that you find attractive—but more
than anything else, finding the right mate is about getting your needs met. When you consistently meet the
wrong men, you have to ask yourself what your role is in
unearthing these unworthy fools.

Are you looking in the wrong places? Are your goals
out of whack? When you keep having the same negative dating experiences, at some point it's time to sit down
and evaluate *you*. Why? Because you are attracting the
qualities in a man that you yourself are exuding. When
you have a healthy assessment of who you are and what
you want out of a relationship, you'll begin to attract like-

minded people. And once you've experienced the way this clarity positively impacts your own well-being, you'll be able to recognize the duds right away and say, "Thank you, but no."

ACT THE LIFE YOU WANT, SPEAK TO THE FUTURE YOU SEEK

*B*efore my husband met me, most of his girlfriends looked like a cross between Michelle Obama and Kenya Moore—dark-skinned, five feet ten inches, with wiry arms and natural hair, looking like they ran track for FAMU. But if you put all those girls together, Jay's needs would still be unmet. When Jay realized that he needed more than a "look," he had a long talk with his friend Keith, and they both agreed it was time to date differently.

Instead of going to clubs, they started attending events for the Congressional Black Caucus and the Association of Black Women Lawyers. As fate would have it, Jay met an amazing woman (who is *everything* packed into a five-foot-three-inch frame and the color of coffee with heavy cream), and although she was unlike the rest, she was simply the best! Okay, I'm talkin' about me—don't hate!

It wasn't that Jay took a long time to realize that what he wanted most was a woman who was caring, funny, down-to-earth, and family-oriented; it just took him a long while to figure out that she might look different than he'd imagined. Instead of going for the look first and hoping that the rest of his priorities would fall into place, he flipped the formula and found that once his priorities were met, his eyes were completely opened—and aroused—by a totally different kind of wrapping!

CHECK YOURSELF

To move forward at any stage of our lives—whether we're single, married, or somewhere in between—we need to regularly check in with ourselves the way a supervisor at work might. It's important that we make time to set goals, evaluate how we're meeting them, and discuss whether they need recalibrating. It sounds silly, but I like to make daily and weekly appointments with myself to keep my agenda on track. They're like beauty appointments for your brain. Awareness is the first step in building the life you want.

CREATE AN "I WANT" JOURNAL

If awareness is the first step toward living your best life, mindfulness is the second step. And when I write things down, they seem more real to me. As it's written in the Bible, "Write the vision and make it plain." So to make my goals and desires a priority, I keep them in the front of mind by taking a few minutes each day to write them down. I start every sentence with "I want" and spend about two minutes writing a stream-of-consciousness list of my desires. I don't even reread the list; I just write it down over coffee in the morning. It is a powerful

tool: ask and you shall receive. And it's easy! Try keeping a running list with a nice mix of frivolous wants and bigger life visions, balancing out stuff like "I want a better relationship with my father" and "I want to stop eating my weight in guacamole while my husband's watching the game."

GET GRATEFUL

Oprah wasn't the first woman with a good weave to recognize the importance of gratitude—and I'm not either. But we can both agree that taking time before bed to isolate one moment from the day that you most appreciate helps us recognize and organize those things in life that make us happiest and most fulfilled. If you write them down, go back and review them to see what patterns emerge—you'll be more likely to have these happy moments when you know what you're seeking.

THROW YOUR BODY INTO IT

I know I'll never have a size two body no matter how many trainers, nutritionists, and witch doctors I hire, but I know that mind, body, and spirit are all closely connected. Exercise such as biking, spinning, or running not only focuses your body on improving itself, it gets your head in the game, too. In the world

we live in, exercising is one of the few times in the day that you can be truly alone with your thoughts—which can be scary! But it's also useful in helping to distill your priorities.

PUT A LITTLE LOVE OUT THERE

Acts of kindness don't need to be random, and they don't need to blow people's minds either. Simply commit yourself to finding one moment in the day when you have the opportunity to be helpful or generous of spirit—to friends and strangers alike. The energy you're putting out in the world comes back to you tenfold. So go on and let that big-ass SUV merge in front of you when you're trying to get to work, and tell the checkout girl at the supermarket that her nails look good. Let the sun shine in and it will surround you wherever you go.

cheat SHEET

I've just laid some serious wisdom on you. Here's a summary of what you need to take with you before moving on to the next chapter:

- ✓ You are in charge of the energy you put out into the world, and you will get what you give.

- ✓ You can't trust the decisions you make when you make them in a broken place.

- ✓ Opening yourself up to love requires opening yourself up to pain.

- ✓ Don't mistake your preferences in men for your priorities. (Note: preferences are those things that you think really matter, but haven't done you any good yet.)

- ✓ Speak to the life you want, say it until you see it, and only surround yourself with people who deserve what you have to give and freely give back.

chapter two

YOU DON'T HAVE TO EAT A WHOLE SIDE OF COW TO KNOW THAT IT'S BEEF

Well, look at you, girl! Now that you've got your head in the game, whether you've got one man in your sights or you're juggling a few contenders at once, this is the fun part; this is the time to enjoy yourself. But dating can be tricky, so you also need to keep your wits about you.

I don't mean to be a buzzkill, but just because you've got your priorities figured out doesn't mean you will always see to it that they're all met, even though you know better. Sometimes it's more fun to be impulsive, which is fine as long as you can tell the difference.

This is *not* the time to forget everything you just learned—especially not the central message of this book: be honest with yourself. It's far too easy to get lost in the excitement of meeting someone new, and I'd hate for you to lose sight of all the priorities you've just determined for yourself. Your perseverance on this path will be tested early on in the dating game; romance trouble doesn't hide out for long, and the strongest offense is a good defense (damn if spending Sundays watching games with Jay didn't teach me something!).

I'm not here to give you a list of ways to fool a man into thinking you're something you're not. The work you're doing isn't about changing who you are; it's about fully recognizing who you are as a person, determining what kind of man is best suited to you, and finding the shortest distance between two points—you and him.

Am I my sister's keeper? Yes, I am—even if we are both trying to "keep" the same guy. Once I even ended up consoling a woman who was in a relationship with the same man I was! I won't get into how it happened, except to say that I knew about her and I thought she knew about me, and when she didn't, it led to a bigger wake-up call for her than me when she rang me up at three in the morning.

At first she demanded to know all sorts of things—if I knew about her, if I knew that they were engaged, if we were sleeping together—before she got to the real doozy, which made me finally stop her: "I'm so pretty! Did you know I'm Puerto Rican? Everyone tells me I'm pretty, and when we walk into a room, heads always turn, and I know we're going to have the prettiest babies! Plus, he told me he doesn't even like black women because they wear weaves and too much makeup and talk too loud!"

"As pretty as I'm sure you are, it's still bought you a one-way ticket into the middle of his b.s.," I said calmly. "Now, as far as this black woman nonsense goes: I'm black. I've got a full head weave, a face full of makeup, and you know how loud I am, and I can't keep his ass from being over here. If you thought you were going to have babies with this man, and if that's what you want, it sounds like you were the only one taking your relationship seriously. If he led you to believe that he wanted kids, then your beef is with him. Or maybe it's a matter of looking at how clear you've been with your intentions—with him and with yourself."

Sometimes I lay the tough love on a little thick when I'm trying to help people see their truest self in the mirror. The sister-girl in me wanted to yell, "Yeah girl, I'm dating your man!" and talk crazy before hanging up the phone on her, but the woman in me heard her brokenness, and I thought, *Whether or not you make it work with this man, if your goal is to be married and have a baby, then you better tell somebody.* So I continued softly as she sobbed, "I know that you're serious about this relationship, but a man who's playing you behind your back when you've expressed to him that you want to have his babies is not going to give them to you very readily or responsibly. Why waste your time when you owe yourself and your babies more?" Then I prayed for her. I know. Crazy, right? Who prays for the other woman? Me, I guess. Since she was in her late thirties, I asked the Lord to hold the gates of her womb open a little while longer because, honestly, I didn't know what else to say. Society tells us that when the other woman calls, we're supposed to say something slick, get in a good dig and cuss her out, but I invite women to think differently, to think of us as a sisterhood. When we see another woman being wronged by someone, can we still be our sister's keeper and help her to see herself more clearly? Yes, we can do that.

Right after we got off the phone, she called me back and asked if we could be friends because when she tried to talk to hers about him they just called her stupid, and her mother refused to discuss it. This is not the point of the story where I tell you that she's sitting up by my pool right now and I'm the godmother of her babies, but I didn't leave her hanging. Instead I left her with this: "If you're at a point in your life where you want to find a man to be the father of your children, you need to be woman enough to make a decision that you can stand by, because that's the only way you will get your needs met.

You'll have plenty of time to worry about someone else's needs later. Trust me. So sit back and enjoy the novelty of putting your needs first. Because there will come a time when you won't have that luxury. Now is the time to focus on your priorities. The worst relationship you can possibly find yourself in is one in which you're in it for him, he's in it for him, and no one's in it for you.

Those days are over, girl. You have way too much self-respect to settle for someone too selfish to love you the right way. You've got two feet; there's the door; no one's stopping you from walking out on a man unworthy of your love. And for those of you whose hearts are racing at the thought of saying good-bye to yesterday, I'd ask you to change your mind to thinking of it as saying hello to your future—the future that you deserve. God is not the author of confusion, and He isn't going to bless a mess.

And don't be hard on yourself for not realizing it sooner, either. When you open yourself up to the possibility of love, you have to be willing to be vulnerable. And that's when things may slip into your blind spot. Being open to love doesn't mean you need to take the next man to send you flowers. Just don't get caught up in the newness for so long that you lose sight of your priorities.

Focus on what you want and ask yourself if he passes muster in the areas most important to you. As long as you pay attention to the warning signs at the beginning of the ride, you'll know to get off long before throwing up. That's progress in my book!

DON'T GO CHASING FOOLISHNESS JUST BECAUSE YOU RECOGNIZE IT

I've *never* understood that notion of sticking with the devil you know. I recognize him, all right—that's why he's not getting up in here!

But I'd be lying if I said I've always been this clear. When I married my first husband, I was twenty-one years old—we were so young that I still smelled like Similac when I was walking down the aisle. We've grown into much better people now and we've both become more self-aware. But in the beginning of that marriage, the fighting started almost immediately, and instead of being concerned, I found myself thinking we were doing what was expected. When I heard him yelling, "Don't you know how much I love you?" and when I looked at him jumping up and down and hollering like a fool, all I could think was *Oh, he must really love me.*

How is that? Because that's what I watched my mother and daddy do the entire time I was growing up. When I think of my parents together, all I can hear is my daddy yelling, "I love you so much. And look at what you're making me do!" They would fight so long and so hard—all in the name of love. So that's what love looked like to me.

After my divorce, when I took a good look at the direction I wanted my life to go in, I put together a list of the qualities my ideal man would have, and I remember thinking, *Oh, I'd love to date a man who doesn't like to fight.* While that was just one quality in a long list of priorities, large and small, it was always right near the top of my list. Argumentativeness was a deal breaker with several guys I met.

When Jay and I hit our first rocky patch, I wasn't entirely sure how to handle myself, so I started carrying on the way I was accustomed to behaving with men in the past. But before I had the chance to get too worked up, Jay calmly said to me, "Why are you talking like that?

I'm not going to try to fight with you. Come sit here next to me and tell me what's wrong. You're so sharp and so quick with your words, I can't think fast enough to keep up."

I'd never been so turned on by a man in my life!

It doesn't matter what kind of bad behavior it is; too often women find themselves enduring the same types of guys repeatedly, simply because they think that since they recognize it, they can handle it; or, worse still, women find a false sense of comfort in the familiar because they don't believe they deserve better. Making a mistake is nothing to be ashamed of—sometimes mistakes are the best teacher and you shouldn't feel foolish because you've been socialized into believing that a certain behavior is acceptable. The trouble comes when a repeated mistake becomes a lifestyle—same song, different verse, and the next time it's always worse!

STICK TO YOUR GUNS

*I*t does not take long to find someone when you're honest with yourself about two things: what you want and what you need. As long as you know which qualities in a man are most important to you and can identify which needs he fulfills, you'd be surprised how many possibilities suddenly open up. It's a simple matter of ask and ye shall receive.

Not long ago a friend came to me in a lot of pain because her expectations were not being met by her boyfriend. She felt that he wasn't as committed to the relationship as she was, and she also hated how he refused to go to church with her. So I said, "Hold up, isn't this the same man who said when you first met that he wasn't interested in anything serious, didn't want a relationship, and had no desire to be married?"

She conceded that he had laid all of that out at the beginning, and they'd had a perfect relationship—until she fell in love with him. When she told him, "Well, I love you now, so we should start talking about what we're doing," his response, point-blank, was, "I already kinda said what I had to say." She was so angry, calling him a liar and saying he had no integrity when he didn't change his mind the same way she did about their relationship. Which I had to point out was unfair. . . .

She wanted all of us girls to be like "Look at how he's doin' you! And you paid for his head shots, you helped him catch up with his bills, and you always pay when you go out, because he's a 'starving artist.'" I had to cut everyone else off and say, "Girl, I love you enough to tell you the truth. That man didn't do anything wrong, and you need to knock it off. He was honest about what he wanted and he's never wavered. If anything, you should have more respect for him than for the man who just tells you what he thinks you want to hear."

She was crushed, devastated. Then I asked her to

trace back to the first time he let her down. "I started asking him to take me to church and he never would. Finally, when I asked him why, he said, 'Because I know how much you love church, and I know what that will mean to you. And it's not gonna mean the same thing to me.'" This man couldn't have been clearer with his intentions. If she'd only been honest with herself when she noticed her own needs shifting, she could have gotten off the ride before she felt that she'd invested far more of herself than she should have. It took exploring her own needs and insisting they be met for her to figure out that it was her time to leave. Sadly, it took her far too long to get there, because she really wanted the relationship to work.

Unfortunately, so many women fall into the trap of giving men too many chances simply because they want a man, so they end up making bum deals with themselves. "I know I said I really wanted a man with a good job, but, shoot, girl, he's gorgeous and he's trying. So I'm going to see if my brother can maybe find a job for him at his company."

When you try to convince yourself that you're okay with things that aren't acceptable to you, you're just stringing *yourself* along. Eventually these shortcomings will let you down, and you will only have yourself to blame. Once I had a girlfriend calling me to say how excited she was about a new man in her life. "Oooh, he's so handsome and fun. I just met all of his friends at an industry party. I'm not into drugs at all. He's just a casual user, he's not addicted though, so we gonna try to ride it out. Once I get him to let go of that we're gonna be good." Then, the next thing you know, she's giving up her Sunday night to go to his group meetings, and she's watching him weave leather into a belt on family night in rehab when she should've been getting herself together in hip-hop zumba. And she's asking herself, *How did I get here?* Well, it's because she compromised at the beginning on things that she already knew were nonnegotiable just because she didn't want to be by herself.

This is not to say that you cannot love a man who has struggled with addiction, or that people aren't capable of bettering themselves—but she should not have been surprised or confused when she found herself in the position she was in. Now she was forced to figure out how important this man was to her, to question what other parts of his person she might also have been letting slide simply in the interest of having someone to spend Sunday nights with.

Just because a man is better than the ones who have shown up before him doesn't mean he's the best for you. . . . This one's only been to jail two times. This one's only got three baby mamas. This one only asks to use my car on the weekends, and he always brings it back Monday before I've got to go to work. These things do not make him the best. It just means he's better than the rest.

I fully understand that we all can't bounce from super-serious relationship to superserious relationship. Between my first husband and my second, I dated half a dozen men, and while they all weren't dream dates, they *were* all progressively closer to the kind of man I was ultimately looking for. If you can do that and chart that for yourself, you know you're on the right track.

When you learn something about a potential love interest early on that does not jibe with the direction you want for your life, you have a choice to make. You can use that information to restore you or destroy you. Oftentimes there is a big chasm between our heads and our hearts, but you need to do what's right, not what feels good, and if your actions don't line up with what you say you want, then there's a lie. It's like your girlfriend who says she wants to lose fifteen pounds but is still running over to the Cheesecake Factory after work. Your actions have to line up with your goals—it's that simple.

ONLINE DATING SECRETS UNLOCKED— IT'S ALMOST TOO EASY!

After my divorce in 2006, I didn't wait long to jump online. I hadn't been in the dating game since the early nineties, and I saw the Internet as a wonderfully efficient way of sorting through a hundred times as many men as I could instead of waiting on blind-date setups and lame happy hours. So I signed up everywhere—Match.com, ChristianSingles.com, BlackPeopleMeet.com, Women WithWeavesLookingForAGoodMan.org . . . do you hear me when I say *everywhere*? It didn't end up being my path to meeting a husband, but I learned a lot about online dating. First up, of course, is how to write your own profile.

1. Don't do this alone. When you're crafting your page, get together with a girlfriend or, better yet, a guy friend, and use them as sounding boards. They should be able to help you identify things that make you attractive to other people. Confidence is key when it comes to selling yourself, so make sure to use supportive friends who will build up your confidence and help you share the best version of yourself.

2. Get specific. When you say things like "I love travel" or "The kitchen is my favorite room in the house," you aren't trying hard enough. Give guys something substantial to sink their teeth into. "Just got my first passport last year for a trip to Costa Rica and would love to check out South America next. Suggestions welcome!" or "Love teaching friends how to make my grandmother's Italian recipes from scratch." A lot of times, guys want to reach out to a woman but they don't know where to start. Make it a little easier on them by providing some interesting personal details and a context that make it easier for their personalities to shine through with a creative response.

3. Beware of clichés. Your profile should be chapter-length, not so long that it's an entire novel. Avoid saying such generic things that could be true of you, your garbageman, and anybody else with a pulse. Everyone loves to laugh, most people find family important, and even liars say they value honesty! Talk about your favorite class at the gym, what your favorite restaurant is, how you'd love to spend this New Year's Eve—provided you have genuine answers. The key is to identify things about yourself that make you different from the last girl whose profile a guy read.

4. Keep it positive. If you're over the drama, if you can't believe you're on this website, if you just got out of a relationship, or you haven't had much luck with the whole dating thing, keep it to yourself for now. If you're trying to move forward, don't talk about disappointments from your past. Chances are the guys reading your profile haven't had flawless dating lives, either. That doesn't mean you need to commiserate with them.

5. Go easy on the demands. It's fair to list some key things you want out of a potential mate, but be careful not to sound demanding. You may not like guys with beards, men under five feet nine inches, guys who didn't go to college, but you can determine all these things from reading his profile alone. Use this opportunity to lay out less obvious priorities he can respond to: "Want to meet someone whose idea of the ideal vacation is more about relaxing on the beach than exploring a new city." "Hoping to find someone who knows which wine to order but isn't afraid to ask for directions if we get lost." "I love catching the game on Sunday, but making it to church in the morning is just as important to me." Less superficial-sounding statements say as much about you as they do about the man you hope to meet.

Just because you've perfected your profile doesn't mean all the heavy lifting's done. Figuring out how to read his profile is just as important as knowing how to write yours.

1. Skip the photos at first. At the beginning of your search, try to jump right into reading profiles without going through all of their pictures. Don't worry, you'll eventually get to see how the guys look, but you should be reading profiles without any preconceived notions about looks. This way, you won't eliminate an otherwise great catch who may not look like someone you'd typically date— *and* you won't cut any cuties too much slack for things in their profiles that will ultimately turn you off.

2. Trust your instincts. We can only do so much about our looks, but we have a lot of control over what we write. If someone sounds a certain way on the page, chances are he's going to come off that way and then some in person. Does he seem arrogant? Nerdy? Shy? Boring? If any of these are no-go's for you, you may need to move along. He's read what he's written several times, and whether or not he's a good writer, he's probably confident with the version of himself that he's tried to put out there. If something sticks out as unappealing to you, it probably won't be less apparent when you meet him.

3. Look for inconsistencies. Once you've found guys whose profiles pique your interest, you can look at the photos. The background of his photos will almost always confirm whether he's telling the truth in his profile. If he says he loves to travel and all of his photos look as if they were taken in his apartment, we may have a problem, Houston. If he says he's social but only has self-portraits taken in the bathroom mirror, you gotta wonder why he couldn't find even one friend to take his picture. If he says he has a great career, or that work is important to him, but he's rocking jean shorts and a Giants jersey in every shot, he may not be the mogul-in-training that he claims to be.

4. Get on the phone. First face-to-face dates can be a major waste of time and a good outfit. Why spend time getting your hair right and your hard-earned money on first-date Spanx and the price of gas traipsing across town only to learn within five minutes of meeting a guy that you'd rather be in line at the DMV? Get your sweatpants on, put a scarf on your head, pour yourself a glass of chardonnay, and have a phone date first. It's not foolproof, but if you've had a good phoner first, the chances of the wheels popping off the bus are far less likely than when going into a date cold. (And texting doesn't count—if you think I'm funny, I need to hear your laugh, not see your emoticon.)

lost in TRANSLATION

ONLINE SPECIAL

When she says, "Relationship-oriented"—
She means "Scram if you're just looking for a hookup."

When he says, "I'm a workaholic"—
He means "If you want someone who will be home for dinner every night, I'm not your man."

When she says, "My family is everything to me"—
She means "You better be ready for a lot of Sunday-night dinners with my mama."

When he says, "I like a woman who takes care of herself"—
He means "If you have ten pounds you've been meaning to lose, let me know when you do."

When she says, "I like staying in as much as going out"—
She means "I prefer staying in."

DON'T FEAR COMPETITION; JUST KEEP YOURSELF IN THE ROTATION

When I told you about the day I met my husband Jay, I may not have told the entire story, so allow me to elaborate on some of our less romantic details.

Before the heavens opened up and angels started singing the moment our eyes locked on the dance floor, Jay and I didn't exactly hit it off. My friend had introduced us at the bar, where we spoke for five minutes and covered all of the important bases (commitment, kids, the importance of family). I had no doubt that I had charmed him, but I had reservations. In that first conversation, Jay came across as serious, and I needed to know that he could open up and have a good time with me, so we made a date to meet on the dance floor later.

When I circled back to my friend, I had just started telling her that I thought Jay was just okay when my friend pointed over my shoulder with her jaw dropped. "Excuse me!" she shouted. "Who's that bitch talking to your new husband?" I turned around to see Jay laughing with another woman, and not in any forced or fake way. He clearly had no problem letting loose with her!

Something I didn't expect came over me. "You're right. That *is* my new husband. The question is, who is that bitch, and why is he laughing with her? I *know* she can't be funnier than me." In that moment, I knew Jay would by my man, and if he was going to laugh hard with any woman, it was going to be me.

So, was it love that brought Jay and me together, or was it competition? I would say that initially it was competition, but so what? Competition starts the day you come into the world, but it is not something to be feared. There's only one line-leader in kindergarten, there's only one captain of the cheerleading squad in high school, and in Destiny's Child there was only one Beyoncé. Once you accept that competition is a powerful force in the world, you have to make it work *for* you, not against you.

When it comes to finding a man who wants to commit, I've found competition can be the most effective way of taking things from zero to sixty. I've never had to tell any man that I didn't want him to date anyone but me—the men have always come to me first. And before you start thinking, *Well, that's easy for her to say, she's a celebrity*, let me remind you that Hollywood's most beautiful woman, Miss Halle Berry, has had her share of man trouble. But if you use competition effectively, any one of you can get a man to have "the talk" long before you make the mistake of trying to have that conversation with him when he's not ready. Let me explain.

When I first started dating Jay, I told him to keep on dating whomever else he was seeing. I said, "I appreciate the fact that the right woman for you will be like cream—she will rise to the top. And if that person is me, so be it. But I'm not going to come in here and ask you to shut your roster down and make you stop seeing these women. What if I'm the wrong girl?"

Well, he thought he'd just landed the best business deal of his lifetime. That's when I gave him the clincher that gave him real pause. I was like "Hold on, handsome, you do realize that's a two-way street, right? Until we're exclusive, if you run into me out or I run into you out, we'll just nod, wave, and keep on going." Talk like that made him want to figure out what he wanted a lot quicker. But you can't make a grown man do anything he doesn't want to do. And if you could, you probably wouldn't want him anymore.

So telling a man that you only want him to date you is a moot point unless he already wants that, too. Monogamy has to be a choice. Every pot has its lid, and if you navigate the world believing that you are a perfect fit with someone, you will find him, he will choose monogamy, and he will choose you. Don't make the mistake of thinking your role in this is passive, however.

As women, we have so much power at the beginning of a relationship, but too often we surrender it. If you're dating a man who knows that you want him to be monogamous, he knows that he can get sex from you because you're looking for something from him. But if you say, "Listen, whomever you're dating, keep dating them. And if you feel like you want to make me more permanent, let me know and we can talk about it." Now the pressure is off you have to have sex with him—he has other women on the team to fill that role, so let him go use them up and save you the headache.

And now, because sex is not clouding your view, you can see the relationship potential clearly. As much as men hate to admit it's true, nine times out of ten it's the girl who isn't putting out that he'll start checking in on.

But again, make no mistake—waiting on you doesn't mean he's waiting. When a man is courting you and you're not sleeping with him, that does *not* mean he isn't being slept with. Men can have sex with a woman as if they're going to the gym—they get a workout in, rest up, take a shower, and walk out with a spring in their step. It takes a guy a hell of a lot longer to start daydreaming about what his kids with you would look like and whether you would take his last name.

Just know that while you view his sexual longing as an emotional investment, he sees it as a physical sport. The good news? He's likely not emotionally invested in any of the women he's sleeping with. But when it comes to a real relationship—it's no game at all, and I'm tired of this notion that we need to play the other person, or that there's some trick to it all. For me, the most successful way to move along from fooling around to getting serious is by approaching the whole thing with the sensibility of a Fortune 500 CEO—putting the business of monkey business first, if you catch my meaning. Which means clearly identifying what you want, focusing on sealing the deal, and making choices based on the highest returns for the corporation that is you.

FIGURE OUT WHY
YOU'RE HAVING SEX
BEFORE THE SPANX COME OFF

$\mathcal{S}$ex doesn't change him, it changes you. When determining the right time to have it, I have only one hard-and-fast rule: don't base your decision on how many dates you've been on or the number of weeks or months you've been together. When you try to eliminate emotions from your decision making, you should at least use your head. When emotions weigh heavily, as they should when it comes to sex, an arbitrary timetable might leave you holding out longer than you need to *or* giving it up before you're good and ready. You can't help what your emotions tell you to do, but don't be impractical and try to override them with a decision determined by some random number that could be applied to anyone's situation—that's a nonsensical way to make a call about something as personal as when, with whom, and how you're going to have sex. Before you drop your drawers, here are a few things to consider:

1. Does having sex go against what I believe? There is such a chasm between sex and religion, and if you have strong beliefs, sex before marriage can leave you with a hearty helping of guilt. While some "church girls" convince themselves that God looks the other way when they're in love, if you decide to go outside the will of your beliefs, you need to be okay with that choice instead of trying to justify it. If you can't, stay in your lane and do what you know is right for you. A suitable man who respects how important this is to you will present himself in time.

2. Are you doing this for you or him? The moment you feel yourself justifying having sex when it's not something you're ready to do, you're in the wrong place. And if it's just because you've never done it before or it's been too long since you've gotten some—girl, they make toys for that.

3. Are you having sex with him because you're worried someone else will? When you are dealing with someone who isn't willing to give you what you want (monogamy), the scales are already tipped—and not in your favor. Why would you give him something that *he* wants—for free—in the hopes that he'll change his mind?

4. Is it just about getting your back broke in bed? Sometimes fair exchange is no robbery, and if it's sex for the sake of sex that you're both looking for—one and done and without cuddling afterward—carry on, I say! Just be sure that's all you want. Sex has to be entered into with careful, honest consideration of how you're going to feel afterward.

SEX WITH YOU IS NOTHING NEW

$\mathcal{S}$ex is not going to make anybody love you or want you more. You can skip to the next chapter now if you want, because it's a simple as that. Since Sodom and Gomorrah people have been convincing themselves that what they've got in their pants and the game they're throwing in bed is somehow different or mind-blowingly better than that of anyone else who's gone before them. But do you honestly think that the average forty-year-old who has been having sex since he was fifteen is going to get with you and instantly decide that it's the best he's ever had and change his intentions? Nay, I say. You can file that under *things that will never happen*.

Eve had everything you've got and Adam still wasn't tending to the garden when that serpent came along. But the biggest gift God could ever give you is a free will. What you do with it, that's on you. My hope is that you'll use this will for things that make you better, not bitter, and that you've participated in a beautiful, loving exchange that you have no regrets about. Anything that will make you feel otherwise? Leave that to those unhappy housewives you see on TV whose lives you love to watch but never want to get messed up in. A woman who's honest with herself is rarely surprised by the situations she finds herself in.

HOMEWORK

Before you hit the next chapter and get it going on out there, you have a few questions to ask yourself first.

► What qualities mean most to you in a man?

► What characteristics have led you to wrong men in the past?

► What ways of meeting a man that you haven't tried are you going to consider?

WHERE TO FIND A GOOD MAN

No one is holding a high heel to your head and forcing you to hit happy hour, girl. Bars aren't the only places to meet a mate—try some of these on for size!

THE GROCERY STORE

We all gotta eat. and most people go to the grocery store solo, which means less distraction for everyone. Ask a man to help you get something off a top shelf. If you play it right, he could be helping you carry those bags to your car—and maybe unloading 'em back at your place, too!

ANY SPORTING EVENT

Whether you hit an actual game or a get-together at someone's house, act interested in what's going on and show you've put in an effort to look good. (That means no jerseys, ladies!) The men usually turn out in packs, and though the male-to-female ratio is always going to be in your favor, it's important to set yourself apart. Just don't stand between him and the game for too long. And remember, at halftime, the team may be off the field, but this is game time for you—a break in the action is

the perfect time for you to shift his focus onto you. This is not the time to give your mama a call or to text your girlfriends. It's crunch time!

AROUND A BODY OF WATER

Whether you're at a hotel pool, a backyard party, or the beach, when people are on the water, they're usually relaxed and approachable. Plus, everyone is in a bathing suit, which means you get to see most of the goods right off the bat!

A WEDDING

Everyone is ripe for the picking with all that romance in the air, and everyone feels like automatic friends at the reception. People's personalities emerge pretty quickly when the music starts—is your man a peacock on the dance floor or is he the cute wallflower in the corner? Either way, weddings are an organic place to meet men, especially because they've been pre-vetted by your friends, too, which is an added bonus. Just make sure you don't pull any antics that will upstage the bride! Move that action off the dance floor, please!

cheat SHEET

I told you I wanted to make this easy on you. Let's do a quick chapter review:

- ✓ You don't need to go all in to know whether someone is the man for you.

- ✓ Following a fool you recognize is no better than flying blind. When you determine the man you want to find, he will eventually present himself.

- ✓ When you identify what Mr. Right looks like to you, it's much easier to not get distracted by guys who aren't him.

- ✓ Competition can be your friend once you accept it as part of the process.

- ✓ That's right—it's a process, not a game.

- ✓ The only person who knows if and when you're ready to have sex is you—screw anyone else's rules.

chapter three

STOMACH FULL,
PENIS EMPTY

As I mentioned, I originally wanted to call this book *Stomach Full, Penis Empty*, but I decided not to give *everything* away on the front cover. Because if I have learned one thing about men, it's fill them with food and empty them of seed regularly and you've got a happy man. It's that simple! Whether you are looking for a man, trying to catch one, or working to keep one, this much is true: if his stomach and his penis are both getting enough attention, he's going to be game for just about anything you want in return.

For some reason, we've been duped into thinking that men are difficult and we are the ones who've got it all together. Hell no! A thousand times no! We women are complex creatures, driven by emotion and thought. Can we be real for a second, ladies? Enough with the notion that men are some inexplicable creatures that are difficult to figure out. Let's be honest—men are easy! We're the tricky ones, driven by emotion and thought. We expect our man to be tough one minute and strong the next, hard-working during the day, but home early when we need him at night, wild on Monday, respectful on Tuesday. But why do we want him to figure out what we want on his own when it would be easier on both of us to just tell him? Guessing games rarely have a winner, and men hate playing them more than you do. Leave it up to chance and who knows what you're gonna get. Ask and ye shall receive is what I say. I love that men are simpler than we are—don't tell them this, but when it comes to your happiness, they're starved for some direction. So why not give it to them? I'm glad a quick BJ or a plate of ribs can turn a frown upside down—or explain away a credit-card bill. When you've blown it, sometimes you just gotta blow it! Are you feeling me? Getting a man's attention doesn't require Jedi mind tricks. If your guy gets upset with you, just take your top off, start rubbing some lotion on your arms, and *boom!* Your nakedness will distract him and deflate his anger. You may like to read the fine print, but most of the time all he needs is a juicy headline to pick up what you're putting down.

Men are visual, so you need to appeal to primal instincts to achieve maximum results. When a man sees you, he'll take all of you in from head to toe, but they approach love from the bottom up—which is to say that at first they think with their penises, determining whether they're sexually attracted to you. If he likes what he sees, he'll be drawn to you—and if he stays at it long enough, he may start to catch feelings in his heart. Only *then* will he make a decision with his big head about whether he can see turning the sex with you into a more meaningful relationship.

Women are the exact opposite. A man could be overweight, too tall, too short, too this, too that, but if he's talking right, if he's captured her thoughts and her mind, she'll want to continue hearing what he has to say and spend more time getting to know him. And the more she talks to a man and enjoys his company, the more her feelings start to grow—and only after she feels something in her heart does she decide to give a man the good stuff. Bottom line, women fall for men from the top down—with our hearts and minds—whereas men usually fall for women from the bottom up, through hunger and libido.

Unfortunately women are ill prepared for (and, often, in denial about) men's motivations—hopefully, I have cleared up that mystery for you. Meanwhile, we women tend to expect things that have never even crossed our man's mind—yet we still expect him to intuit our needs just as we have his. The trouble is, our needs are usually subtler and therefore more complicated than his, so we need to communicate clearly; otherwise our men will continually disappoint.

It all comes down to how men and women are wired. In one corner you have a species whose decision making is based on critical thinking, and in the other, you have a species whose actions are governed by emotions. Which isn't to say that our emotions are invalid, but I will say that they are often unreliable and sometimes counterproductive.

Men are so simple, so primal, that they're almost exclusively led by what gets them fed and what gets you in bed. Now, that may sound reductionist, but trust me, it's true. And that's a good thing, ladies, because when you accept that truth, you will *never* be confused by their actions again. We're the ones who complicate things when we try to imagine that their minds work any differently. But when you recognize this truth and exploit it for your own gain rather than fighting nature, you will always be in pole position in your relationship.

And speaking of pole position, I think it's time to get into the nitty-gritty just a bit here. In my house, Jay and I have a morning routine that some of you may find shocking. Some of you may even think my husband is in charge based on this routine, but that's where you'd be wrong. You see, my husband is lucky to be awoken by a special rise-and-shine every morning—yes, ladies, every morning, and yes, that kind of rise-and-shine. We call it the "alarm cock." Now, I know a lot of you are thinking, *Every day, girl? Damn, Jay is one lucky man.* And you'd be right, because my husband is lucky—*and he knows it.* Why do you think I take care of him in bed every single morning? Because one well-timed blow job and the rest of the day—week, month, year—is mine. Who do you think is in charge now?

If my husband walked in the door right now and I called out for him, he'd say, "Yes, baby. What do you need, beautiful?" And if I reached into my purse and asked him to run around the corner to grab me something, he'd already be out the door. Sometimes I'm just like, "Babe," and he'll hand me his whole wallet when that's not even what I'm asking for.

Why? Because I already laid the groundwork that morning in bed, and he knows what time it is. When you take care of your man's needs regularly, he will be all the more willing to reciprocate: Once that alarm cock goes off in the morning, you won't have to ask him twice to do anything for you. Plain and simple: controlling when, how, and where your man gets his sex is a power play that can never be beat!

DON'T OVERTHINK IT

*H*onestly, we women come into this lovemaking business with so many more hang-ups than the men we're hoping to ensnare. We're in the mirror counting our stretch marks, lamenting that one of our boobs looks smaller than the other, we're sure our behind is sagging more than it did the month before. But my grandmama hit the nail on the head when she told me, "Baby, when you're the only naked woman in the room, you look good!"

For all the talk about being highly visual creatures, and for all the time we spend fretting about whether a particular pair of pants makes us look fat—if we just took our damned pants off, we'd have nothing to worry about. At the end of the day (and at the beginning of it, and in the middle of it) men really just want us naked. While taking care of our bodies is important, it all starts with learning to take care of ourselves by listening to our bodies and treating them in a way that makes us feel good. It's not about conforming to what men want— or more accurately, what you think they want. When we feel good about ourselves, men are generally pretty pleased, too.

When Jay and I first started dating, I was spending more time at Victoria's Secret than Heidi Klum. I've always been a lingerie girl, and I worked that bedroom like a runway in every imaginable combination of bras, panties, teddies, and camisoles. And the harder I tried, the less impressed my husband seemed to get. When he'd say things like "What's this?" and "How do I get this off of you?" all I heard was "You're not sexy." Finally I said to him, "Do you like it when I dress up? Does any of my lingerie turn you on?" And he replied sweetly, "Baby, I love you most when you're fresh out of the tub with nothing but lotion on. Everything else is too complicated and just slows me down."

Well, when I learned that, getting ready for bed got a *lot* easier, and the Salvation Army could have opened up an entire lingerie boutique with the bags of stuff I brought in, because once I learned that nothing got my husband hotter faster than when I got down to my birthday suit, it quickly became the thing I felt sexiest in, too! And what a beautiful thing to love yourself most in your most natural state. I can't stress this enough: these are simple creatures we are dealing with, and you may not need to try nearly as hard as you imagine.

WHEN HE'S RUNNING ON EMPTY, HE AIN'T GETTING VERY FAR

When I talk to women at the beginning of their relationship, one of their biggest worries I hear is that their men are spending too much time away from them. But trying to tell a grown man he can't go somewhere will only make you look like a fool and have him turning on his heel to head for the door fast. I've never told Jay he couldn't go out with his boys—hell, I let him meet them all the time at pro sports skyboxes half-full of groupies. But if he's going out, he's going out empty. Period.

A few months ago, I was on my way home from the studio and I knew my husband was headed to a game that night with the guys, so I called him as soon as I got in the car on the way home:

"Hey, baby, what time you heading out?"

"I'm leaving in about twenty minutes."

"I'll make it home in fifteen."

I pushed that pedal all the way down, and when I got home, he was in the bathroom brushing his teeth and buttoning up his shirt. I stepped right in front of him at that bathroom sink, unbuttoned his pants, and got down to business real quick. Within five minutes we were finished and I was pushing him out the door.

"Dang, girl, my legs are like Jell-O. Do you think I should cancel?"

"Honey, I ironed your shirt. You made plans with your friends. You should go."

After taking the hunt out of him, I knew I had nothing to worry about. I could have wasted my night getting all pissy and riled up thinking about all those skanky women flirting with my man while I sat home in my head scarf and a funky pair of sweatpants, waiting to pounce on him with 150 questions about the girls who were there that night. But a well-timed BJ kept both of us from acting out in ways we'd have wished we hadn't. Instead of being completely irrational, I was the understanding wife, encouraging her husband to spend more time with the guys. And sure enough, by the time he made it to the game, he was already sending me texts like "They've got some great food up here, babe, but I'm beat. I probably won't stay the whole game." It was as if the idea of coming home early were actually his!

I mean, really? Will men ever cease to be predictable? I *hope* not. Jay was back home on the couch with me before the game was over—and you know who was in charge of the remote by then!

IT'S CALLED A BLOW JOB
BECAUSE IT'S WORK

Make sure your weaves are sewn in tight, girls, 'cause we're about to get real here.

There are two times when you should sleep with your partner: when you feel like it, and when you don't. Sex is vital in maintaining a dynamic, lasting relationship—without sex, there's little difference between a husband or a boyfriend and a friend. But we all have moments when we can't be bothered to get naked, and at those times the blow job is your best friend.

Now, I can't very well tell you how crucial blow jobs are to making the world go round without giving you a little technique talk. Here are some tips that cut *you* a little something in the deal.

1. Alarm cock: Is your man heading out of town for a few days? The morning he's leaving, set your alarm fifteen minutes before his and wake him up with an unannounced blow job—you'll be the first thing he thinks of that day and the final thought on his mind when his head hits the pillow that night.

2. Game changer: Whether he's riding high while his team is up at the half or he's tense and cranky if they're down, a midgame blow job will bring his focus back where it belongs—on you. You'll find that he'll be far more likely to focus on you during commercials—and if things go really well, he may even lose interest in the second half altogether!

3. Velvet tongue: Sometimes you're tired and need to get to bed early, so you need a blow job in your tool kit that's fast-acting on him and low impact on you. Tell him to meet you in bed while you fix yourself a cup of hot tea. Take a big sip before you hit the sheets and keep it in your mouth a bit before heading south. The element of surprise along with the heat will send his soldier into immediate salute, and it will be lights out for him *and* you in five minutes flat.

4. Penis colada: When a special occasion such as his birth-day or an anniversary is coming up, tell your man that if he drinks pineapple juice every day for a week, you'll reward him by swallowing. Not only will his sauce taste better, but seeing him work for it all week will make it seem all the sweeter, too.

THINK OF HIS SEXUAL HISTORY AS A PROVEN TRACK RECORD

*B*efore Jay and I got married, we were hanging out checking our Facebook pages when I grabbed his computer and started scanning through his friends. I noticed that many of the women he was friends with looked an awful lot like the type of girl he used to date. Naturally, I couldn't help but wonder how good a friend he was to each of them.

"Tell me something, Tall, Dark, and Handsome. You've got six hundred friends. Now, how many of these women have been your concubines?"

Ladies, let me just say right now that I do not recommend having this conversation with your man unless you're truly ready to hear any possible answer. The number of sex partners he's had will either be too high and you'll think he's a dog, or it will be lower than yours and you'll feel like a slut. We all have a past, and while I'm such a strong advocate of walking in the truth, when you get into that conversation, I feel that the only thing that comes to mind is to lie and lie good.

When Jay told me his answer was forty, whoa. I wasn't upset as much as I was just totally caught off guard and surprised by our difference in numbers. He laughed at first when he saw how shocked I was, so I said, "Well, what would happen if I told you I racked up the same kinds of numbers?"

That's when he admitted that there was a double standard. "I'm not telling you that it's right," Jay said. "But I would be upset and that's just the way it is."

But still, my issue wasn't with the number itself; it was that he was in touch with them, or at least they knew what he was up to for the most part because of Facebook. "Twenty-five of these women can log on to see how you're doing, comment on your status, and weigh in on your day?!"

He had already seen where this conversation was

going, and before I started down a line of further questioning, he said, "It's gone. I just deleted my whole Facebook account. I'm committed to what we're doing, and if any of this gives you a reason to question me, it's done." Without hesitation, he eliminated something that made me feel less than the most important woman in his life.

But I have to thank at least some of these women for preparing Jay to be his most self-aware sexual being. When a man gets married and still has fantasies rattling around in the back of his mind, that doesn't mean they go away. My feeling is, if you need to have a white girl, a black girl, and an Asian, then have a threesome, take a guy trip to Brazil, do whatever you're going to do so that by the time you come to me, all is well and you've satisfied a lot of your curiosities.

Call him a player or call him a man-whore for his behavior before he met you. Just keep in mind that whatever he's done to get those notches on his belt, the truth is, when you're looking to settle down, you want a man with multiple and varied experiences, because the last thing you want is someone whose I-want-to-f#@k-it list is longer than his bucket list.

And it's not just about your man getting certain fantasies out of his system or having had enough women that he feels ready to settle down; it's also about being with a man who has identified the things that satisfy him most. A man who knows what he wants is sexy. Period. Confidence is alluring. And being open and interested in his sexual interests opens the door for him to ask you questions about yours. Without naming names—because it doesn't really matter whom he did what with, he's yours now—it's worth having a transparent conversation about what you want out of your sex life and what fantasies you hope to play out with him. That goes a long way in preventing either of you from pining away for a sexual experience you thought you'd never be able to share with each other and will save you from looking elsewhere.

After Jay got rid of his Facebook page, he did ask one thing of me:

"We're about to get married and yet so many guys have your phone number. I think you should change it."

"Why? I'm friends with everybody I used to date."

"Why is that?" Jay asked.

"I just am. They're there to talk about things that I'm going through, someone to share a laugh with."

"Well, that's what I'm here for. How do you think it's

going to work? Your phone rings on Sunday night while we're in bed and it's one of your ex-boyfriends, and I'm just supposed to sit right there while you talk to him on the phone? That's not going to happen. What are you talking to him about that you can't discuss with me? Tell me the added value."

I gave it a moment's thought and couldn't figure out why I needed to be friends with these five people I'd broken up with—particularly if it hindered my moving forward in my relationship with Jay. Women always hold it as a badge of honor to be friends with all their exes. Finally Jay put it to me another way:

"Anytime you reach back around to a guy you used to be with, even if he knows you're with somebody, he's going to see that as an open door, a chance, a possibility. You may or may not take it, but that's how we see it. 'All I gotta do is wear her down long enough.' Because he has your ear and you're in communication. That's how a man is gonna take that." I changed my number the next day.

There's no sense in hating on those broads you don't recognize on his Facebook page, though—you don't need to take them out for a drink, but you should be thankful that it was them and not you he was tossing up, flip-

ping around, and splitting in half ten different ways till
he found out what he liked. I think that in this day and
age, it's silly for us to pretend we don't have rich sexual
histories, and it would be a shame not to discuss, respect-
fully, what we've learned about ourselves from others. It
doesn't matter where either of you has been if, in the end,
you've chosen one another.

lost in TRANSLATION

When she says, "I've only been with seven guys"—
She means "Technically it's eleven, but I don't count
all of them."

When he says, "I've been with twenty-five women"—
He means "You don't want to know my real answer here."

When she says, "I'm not sure where I learned how
to do that"— She means "Quit asking me about it.
You've met the guy."

When he says, "Do you want to have sex tonight?"—
He means "I want to have sex tonight."

When she says, "Do you want to have sex
tonight?"— She means "Is it time for us to have sex
again tonight?"

TEACH THE OLD DOG
A NEW TRICK

Since I'd spent plenty of time in beauty parlors all over Los Angeles, it only seemed fair that I spend a day at Jay's barbershop to get some intel from men on what they want. Judging by the eager response I got from nearly every guy I spoke to, you'd think they'd been waiting for years to tell women what it is they wish we knew.

They did nothing to convince me they are any less simple than I've made them out to be. But across the board, the thing they think we don't understand is that they actually care whether we're satisfied in the sack—they wish we had more feedback for them. That's right, ladies, they *want* to give us what we want!

One guy admitted, "It's not that we don't care about you having an orgasm—it's just that we're going to have one regardless of whether or not you do. So if you don't tell us what you want, we probably aren't going to bother trying to figure it out. Most guys would be very pleased to know that their lovemaking gave their woman an orgasm. I'd be a lot happier knowing exactly what it is that I'm doing right so that I can keep at it and get us both a happy ending at the same time. It seems like women often assume that they aren't going to climax, so they don't even bother telling us what might actually get them there."

Everyone wants to feel that he or she is doing a good job in bed—which is something to keep in mind if you do choose to enlighten your partner on his moves. Accentuate the positive before you get into what you aren't getting, and the results will be better for everyone involved.

 **REVAMP**

EAT YOUR WAY TO A SPICIER SEX LIFE

The fastest way to a man's heart is through his stomach, especially with foods targeting three specific areas of attraction.

1. Desire. Fire up testosterone levels with foods high in zinc. Because our zinc levels are generally sensitive, just ten or twenty minutes after ingesting it, you'll get a noticeable boost in energy and general sexual interest. We may not still fully know why it is such an important ingredient in the production of hormones; we just know that low levels cause children's sexual development to slow down and men's sperm production to decrease. Some people say this is malarkey, but other people recommend oysters as an aphrodisiac because of their high zinc content—but for the record, frying them kills the effects. And for less decadent foods with just as much zinc, go for a handful of lightly toasted pumpkin seeds or snack on some low-fat roast beef.

2. Arousal. Get blood heading to all the right parts with happy hormones. Peppers give you the same kind of rush that exercise does by pumping endorphins into your body; pine nuts

are loaded with an amino acid that gets your lady parts per-colating and keeps his sperm circulating; and believe it or not, according to Dr. Oz, natural compounds found in watermelon relax blood vessels the same way Cialis and Viagra do, keeping everyone's juices flowing freely.

3. Affection. Now give your body *and* your brain that warm and fuzzy feeling. Chocolate runs a distant second to sex in my book, but eating it does stimulate the same part of your brain. Just keep the cocoa content nice and dark. Reaching orgasm takes many things—but just to get those muscles to contract, your body needs magnesium, something found in high amounts in mozzarella cheese, so grab a couple of cubes! Some studies say it also releases ten times the amount of happy hormones as chocolate. That's *amore*!

cheat SHEET

Keep it simple, sister. Men are only as complicated as we make them. To recap:

✓ Blow jobs and a good plate of ribs can save the world.

✓ Taking the hunt out of a man is as easy as keeping his dragon drained.

✓ Mine your partner's prior sex life for his favorite, time-tested techniques.

✓ Tell him what's working for you in bed (and what isn't). He actually wants to know.

chapter four

HONESTY IS THE
NEW MONOGAMY

One of the most powerful things we have as women is our intuition. It pretty much never fails us—*if* we listen to our guts. When a woman discovers that her significant other has gone outside of the relationship and finds out with whom he had the affair, is she ever that surprised? Come on now. Our intuition warns us that something is going on with him—or with us . . . because it almost always takes two to screw up a relationship—and often that something may always have been there; we just chose to ignore it.

One day, I had this feeling that my boyfriend was up to no good—I don't know exactly what hit me in that moment, but I just knew he was cheating on me. I knew it with everything inside me. His ex-girlfriend was still in touch with him at the time, and I could tell that she was still into him and was trying to gauge whether I would be around for long. So when I tried calling him at home to see what he was up to and he didn't answer the phone, something just snapped in me. I was sure he was with this other girl. It was my woman's intuition. And I needed to see it for myself. Even though I felt it, I needed to confirm it. I had to have that "gotcha" moment.

Blinded by an insatiable desire to prove myself right, I jumped into my car in a complete frenzy. I was determined to get to his house in seven minutes, though it would normally have taken me fifteen. So I'm drivin' like a bat out of hell because I want to see it with my own two eyes. I was *so* obsessed with catching this man cheating that I didn't realize the police had started following me on the freeway. I heard no sirens. I didn't see any cops. The only thing I could do in that moment was just get there.

When I pulled off the freeway, a center divider blocked the turn into his street, meaning I'd have to drive an extra block to make a U-turn. But I was scared that if I drove that far, I would miss catching this girl leaving his house. So, in the heat of the moment, I hopped the curb, ripping out the entire undercarriage of my car.

To say it was an intense situation is an understatement.

I pulled up to his house just in time to see the two of them in his driveway—she was leaning against his car and he was leaning against her as if they were in an ad for some cheap cologne. My worst fear had come true. That's when I heard the sirens and an officer yelling into a bull-horn. With my life flashing before my eyes, I thought, *Oh my God. I cannot go to jail. I'm willing to do a lot for this relationship, but going to jail ain't one of 'em.*

I heard the cops telling me to step out of the car and put my hands up. I moved cautiously so they wouldn't tase me, all the while wondering how I was going to explain myself to the authorities. All they saw was a crazy woman driving a hundred miles an hour and jumping the median. They had yet to see a crazy woman catching her man cheating.

As I stepped out of the car, I saw two police officers— one male and one female. I made a beeline for the lady cop and threw my arms around the back of her bullet-proof vest and started wailing, "Oooh, girl. Look at my man! Look at his ass standing here in broad daylight with some other girl when he is supposed to be with me!" Sob-bing away, I started clinging to this woman as if she were a lifeboat, just wailing and howling, until I felt her put her arms around me. When she started rubbing my back and telling me it was okay, I knew I wasn't going to jail.

I decided to be an actress when I was five years old, but I'm pretty sure this was the moment when I knew an Academy Award wasn't far away.

The whole time I was looking over her shoulder at my man and his side piece with rage in my eyes, mouthing, *You gonna get it!* The police left without giving me so much as a ticket. The universe had opened up and given me the sign I asked for and showed me what I so desperately needed to see.

Intuition is what led me to his house. Anger is what drove me to almost get arrested trying to get my worst fear confirmed. Foolishness is what allowed me to stay even after the affair was confirmed. And do you know what I had the audacity to do after catching him cheating? Instead of slapping the black off him, I stayed with him many more years than I care to admit!

So what good did it do me to go to his house and see it all for myself if I was just gonna stay in the situation anyway? What difference did it make? Except nearly landing me in the slammer, trying to look pretty for my mug shot. Trying to make someone commit to monogamy when the person is clearly not ready, or forcing the situation to be what you want it to be, simply never works out.

Clearly, I was acting on my emotions and not thinking the situation through logically. Had I used logic, I would have driven past, seen him with her, and realized that he didn't want what I wanted because he still wanted two different things, and I should have just let him go on and be. I didn't realize that I couldn't make him choose me. I couldn't force his hand to see that I was the better woman. But having to get out of going to jail with the LAPD, that'll grow you up real quick.

Here's the thing we don't get until it's too late: Marriage is not magic. It does not change people; it only magnifies who they are. We have this crazy notion that once we marry a guy, things are going to be different. "Once I marry him, he's going to behave in a different way. Once I marry him, a different level of respect is going to kick in. Once I've got the ring, these other girls are going to fall by the wayside." That's one of the biggest lies ever told. Yet, there I was . . . wanting to believe that a good man inside him would manifest itself in a different way.

I tell you this story not just because I want to embarrass my ex or to publicly thank the police officer who showed me mercy that day—thank you, girl!—I bring it up because it illustrates four key lessons about infidelity.

1. Your intuition is almost always right.

2. You shouldn't ask any question you aren't ready to hear every answer to.

3. Men and women cheat for very different reasons.

4. Being a victim is a choice.

I believe that a relationship can survive an affair. However—and it's a big however—you must arm yourself with knowledge about where you stand on the subject before you are forced to make a decision about it. If your partner has been dishonest with you, at least be honest with yourself. But let's start from the beginning.

lesson #1:

IF IT WALKS LIKE A DUCK AND TALKS LIKE A DUCK AND LOOKS LIKE IT'S SLEEPING WITH SOME OTHER DUCK, IT'S PROBABLY CHEATING ON YOU

Here's the thing about intuition: God gave it to you for a reason. It can either help if you listen to it, or it can hurt if you end up having the woulda, shoulda, coulda's in the long run. But it's tricky because when you are in love with a man—or a woman; this applies to everyone in a relationship—sometimes you don't want to trust the instincts you have about your partner. Yet, when you have a strong connection with someone, as much as you would like to believe that everything is going smoothly in the relationship, it's hard to be fooled once you are emotionally invested.

When I caught my ex-boyfriend cheating, it wasn't as if I had a crazy vision in the middle of the night or visited a voodoo priestess who shook a chicken carcass over my body and told me my man was being unfaithful; I was no oracle. The signs had been presenting themselves to me for months and months. I just wasn't ready to confront them . . . until I was.

lost in TRANSLATION

When she says, "I don't expect my man to be faithful"— She means "I've been down this road before and I've adjusted my expectations."

When he says, "I can't leave my wife for you"— He means "I can't leave my wife for you."

When she says, "It was nice to talk to someone who really listened"— She means "Damn, I can't get that man outta my head."

When he says, "I'm not sure when I'll be home; stop asking me"— He means "I'm still transitioning into commitment. Give me a minute."

When she says, "Is there something you want to tell me?"— She means "There's a question I want to ask you, and I already know the truth so don't lie."

lesson #2:
CLEAR YOUR THOUGHTS;
THEN FEEL FREE TO
LOSE YOUR MIND

I remember getting a phone call from a girlfriend late one night not long ago.

"Hey, girl. What's going on?" she whispered.

"You tell *me* what's going on. You're the one whispering."

"I'm talking low because I'm in his garage."

"Doing what?"

"Breaking into his phone. I'm trying to figure out the code so I can see who he's been talking to."

"What are you going to do when you figure that out?" I asked.

"Depends on what I find."

Two weeks later, another late-night call:

"Hey, girl."

"Oh, Lord, you're whispering again," I said.

"Yeah, I'm out in his bushes. He's got someone over here."

"I'll try to get there before the police do." I sighed and grabbed my car keys.

By this time, she had already broken into his phone, she had cracked the code on his computer, and she'd even found a letter in the bottom of his gym bag confirming what she already knew. Now she was watching him cheat with another woman from outside his bedroom window. But she hadn't figured out what she wanted to do with this information before she received it. That's why it would take having a few kids, being cheated on several times, and learning he had a child with another woman before she was able to call it quits. She wasn't ready to digest that her man was cheating on her, and she hadn't done the homework on herself to sort out what she was willing to do to move on with her life without him.

Whatever questions you are grown-up enough to ask, you have to be man or woman enough to hear the answers. The problem isn't in asking these questions, mind you. Asking the questions is healthy, and when you are in a healthy relationship, the answers will be honest.

But what happens when your man is not being honest with you and you catch him cheating? Well, I wouldn't recommend getting in a high-speed chase or jumping any medians over him. He is *certainly* not worth that!

But if we don't evaluate how we'd respond to every possible answer in advance, we will be wholly unprepared to respond to whatever curveball is thrown our way. Instead, we're caught off guard and we make choices based in emotion. For fear of losing our man, we make decisions from a broken place, and the consequences will bite you in the ass every time. It's important to know what your plan is if what you think proves to be true.

I stayed with my ex for years before determining that he'd never turn into the man I wanted him to be. So I'm not saying it's easy to break the spell. But only you are in charge of your destiny. And once you start walking in your truth, you will realize that you deserve a hell of a lot more than settling for a man who doesn't show you the love and respect you deserve.

The bottom line is this: whether you are confronting your partner directly or digging up evidence on your own, before you do so, I invite you to have an intimate conversation with yourself about all the possible outcomes, so that you are in a place to receive information intelligently and logically before your judgment gets clouded by emotions. That way, when it is time to make a decision about next steps, you've already developed a game plan with your own best interests at heart and in mind.

BEWARE THE MARRIED MAN

I know so many women who have dated married men. But I am here to tell you that God, the universe, or whatever your higher power is—he's never going to tell you that somebody else's man or woman belongs to you. Nobody's got your husband. If you meet someone who is with somebody else, move it right along, and I say this to protect you as much as him. Because you are going down a path of settling for less than you deserve.

Do you want to celebrate Christmas on December 26? Do you want to miss his birthday because he's with his other family? No. You're the one whose time, mind, and body are getting used up, and you're never going to get the maximum benefit.

lesson #3:
IT'S EASIER FOR MEN TO CHEAT— AND HARDER FOR THEM TO FORGIVE

I'm not saying it's necessarily fair, but it does make sense: men can dish it, but they just can't take it. The first reason for this is primal: men are so territorial by nature, it's much harder for them to get over the notion that another man has *had* their woman. The mere thought cuts them and their pride at the knees. (One conversation you'll never hear between two men: "Dog, she cheated on me, but we're working it out." "Right on, brother. Good luck with that." That conversation ain't never gonna happen.)

And second, men cheat for variety; women cheat for validation. In other words, when men cheat, it's usually just about physical sex. When women cheat, it almost never is. In that sense, it *should* be easier for us to forgive a man, knowing the affair was physical and not emotional, than it is for a man to forgive us. It all comes down to our being much more complicated creatures. Your man could be drunk at a party with some girl backing up on him. He gets aroused, and the next thing you know they're in the bathroom like a couple of horny teenagers.

Your man might never even think of that woman again—men are entirely capable of separating sex and feelings, and sometimes for them it's simply curiosity about what else is out there purely on a sexual, physical level, and once he's had it, he won't need to return to it. But women have a lot of trouble recovering from a man's physical transgression because to her the act has so much more emotional significance.

Women tend to stray with someone who is able to speak into our listening—someone we make an emotional connection with first because they talk to us in a way that appeals to part of our emotional side that's been feeling neglected, someone who seems to understand our feelings better than our man at home does—and generally, this kind of hookup requires a little premeditation. It also means we're probably more mentally engaged in cheating than our male counterparts, who can be completely spontaneous in deciding to stray, and their misdeeds can often be chalked up to a temporary lapse in judgment and quickly forgotten.

When a woman cheats, she's emotionally invested—usually, she's not going out and sleeping with another man just because she wants a new flavor. But if a man has captured her mind and makes her feel something in her heart, by the time she sleeps with him, she's in it to win it, and getting her back is not gonna be easy. Because women's cheating goes that much deeper, it's not only harder for men to forgive us, it's harder for women to leave the affair behind entirely because of that emotional engagement, and that makes it even harder for a man to get that image of your being with another man out of his head—he knows you're invested in it. Even when your part-time lover leaves, you are still playing the movie version of your idyllic time together on a loop in your head, because the idea that someone out there can give you what has been missing in your relationship—whatever it is that your man can't or won't give you—lingers.

Regardless of gender, though, surviving infidelity simply means that you have agreed that you love each other enough to work through the hurt, and that both people in the relationship want to put the affair behind them. The hardest part about getting your relationship back on track isn't about forgiving your mate. The biggest challenge for both parties is to identify how you got to this point as a couple and then to take responsibility for the part you played in allowing your love to be compromised. Because love is the only way to find your way back to one another.

Take my friends Renee and Kevin (whose names have been changed to protect the foolish). Now, while it's true that Kevin was the dog that cheated on Renee, it's possible she could have done some front-end work either to repair the holes in the relationship or to determine that it was time to cut and run. Before you jump all over me for taking his side, let me paint a picture.

On the drive home from work, I got a call from Kevin: "I gotta talk to you right now! Where can I come meet you?" I could tell from the tone in his voice that he had no business being on the road, so I told him to pull over and that I would meet him wherever he was. When I got there, he was pacing as if he'd just killed a man.

"It wasn't something I meant to do. We went for happy-hour drinks after work, and as soon as we got there, this woman started laying it on real thick, telling me how great my presentation was, what a rock star I'd been, and how crucial I was. Then she bought a round of shots and got drunk pretty quickly. She needed a ride home, and all of a sudden her mouth was in my lap."

"I take it you drove her home. And then drove it home to her?"

"No, no. I couldn't do it. Things weren't working down there. I felt too guilty."

"Well, before you do anything, promise me you won't tell Renee what you just told me."

"Too late."

As if doing one foolish thing that day wasn't enough. Listen up, people. No matter how guilty you feel, if you've cheated on your mate and you know you'll never do it again—take that secret to the grave with you. If you've gotten a taste of something on the street and you've been scared straight into not ever going back to that place again, sit and stew on it but keep your mouth shut. You aren't fooling anyone and you're hurting everyone if you think your confession is for your partner's sake. You're only trying to absolve yourself of your guilt—but that guilt is your punishment. If you feel bad about your behavior, take it like a man or a woman, and keep it to yourself. Regardless of what anyone tells you, no one would rather know he or she has been cheated on if he or she doesn't have to—no one.

At this point, though, there was no turning back for these two. It was time to perform relationship triage. Their inability to recognize when and where and how each other's needs weren't being met caused the greatest chasm between them. And that's what makes room for someone else to come in.

Just two weeks before this, Renee and I were discussing a communication breakdown she and Kevin were having. He was a lot like me in craving ear candy—he likes to be complimented when merited, praised for his accomplishments, and thanked for his kindness—and Renee wasn't so comfortable doling out the words he so wanted to hear. My advice was pretty simple: "Get comfortable with it." Instead of appreciating my wisdom, though, she blew me off: "I'm not just gonna turn into the kind of woman who's always doting on her guy. He's a grown man."

And now here we were. Did she wish she'd been more sensitive? Did he wish he'd been clearer about needing more positive reinforcement from her? Hell yes, two times over. But where was this level of transparency? The time to have this conversation isn't when you get caught; it's when you get curious. And by that I mean, when you find your head getting turned more often than it used to, ask yourself why. If it's because you're not getting something from your partner, talk to your partner about it. It might not be an easy conversation to have, but it's far less complicated than the kind that comes with a lawyer attached.

I also asked Renee to ask herself, why, if she doesn't like to constantly shower her guy with affection, would she date someone so clearly into it? I wasn't suggesting that she leave him, but if she did, what would her take-away be? Had she lost men before for lack of affection? If so, was she going after the wrong guys? I told her she didn't need to give me these answers, but she did need to give them to herself so she'd know what to do next. Either way, the choice was hers, and once she understood that, she was empowered to make a decision for herself—and only for herself and her own well-being.

lesson #4

SET BOUNDARIES—AND THEN ACCEPT THAT THOSE BOUNDARIES WILL BE PUSHED

If you say you can handle his stepping out on you, you can damn well count on his doing just that. You basically just wrote him a prescription to. But until you live it, you may think that you'll be fine with his carrying on with other women as long as it's not in your face. Then you come to find out you rip your hair out every night he isn't around, wondering which one of your girlfriends he's with. Just look at the lives of athletes and their wives playing out on TV. These ladies say they know full well what they're signing up for, but then they get mad when it happens. Sweethearts, you have no legs to stand on—in those stilettos these guys paid for.

I have plenty of women friends who believe that men aren't monogamous by nature, and they say that they don't expect their men to remain faithful. What they do expect is that he will be respectful and not flaunt it in their face or embarrass them. To me, though, I feel that most people, at the core of their being, cannot live in that space *just* outside of a monogamous relationship. Because even if you talk a good game, when you find out that somebody else has been invited to the party, something makes you say, "Why wasn't I enough?"

You have to be tired of settling for less. You have to believe that you deserve more. Nobody in the world can want more for you than you want for yourself. I know a lot of women who are beautiful inside and out, but they don't believe that they deserve more than they're getting. So, they just ride out what they've got. When you have a "this is as good as it's gonna get" attitude, then you'll never have the life you want—because if you don't want more for yourself, no one else will either.

lesson #5:
BUT IF YOU'RE IN IT TO WIN IT, LOSE THE INSPECTOR GADGET ACT

*I*f you do decide that you're going to stick it out in the relationship, know that you *truly* have to forgive your man before either of you can begin anew. If you are in that same headspace you were in when you learned you'd been betrayed, you will not be able to put aside your feelings and move forward into a healthy, trusting relationship. If you still feel that you are the victim or that you get to be the angry girlfriend or angry wife forever, the wedge your behavior creates between you and your partner will be larger and even more insurmountable than that created by the act itself.

If you don't think you can trust him and you want

a man who is committed to being wholly monogamous, what are you sticking around for? It's one thing to accept that he's not going to be faithful to you and so you just take from the relationship what you're in it for—be it financial security, status, citizenship, you name it. But if you entered this relationship thinking that once you married him things were going to be different, you have bought into one of the biggest lies ever told. And now that you've seen where it's gotten you, you're going to make yourself crazy if you're constantly creeping around corners, waiting to trip him up once again. Ultimately, the choice is yours, and so is how you conduct your life after making that choice. Remember, you're allowed to change your mind, too.

SEX MISTAKES MOST WOMEN MAKE

We've all made 'em. Here's how to avoid 'em!

Thinking a guy is always ready. I know I told you that all men care about is food and sex. But there are times in the day where he's not always up for either—especially when he's over forty. Always assume he's ready to play, but don't be disappointed or take it personally during those times when he isn't.

Worrying about what you look like. When you and he are actually in the moment, he doesn't give a damn how big your boobs aren't or how lopsided your booty is. By the time you've hit the sheets, he's in it to win it, so feel as confident as you ever have that he's never wanted you more.

Not giving him enough guidance. When it comes to sex, if you don't make what you want clear, he will never know otherwise, so you gotta tell him how your party works. Men may not like to ask for directions, but in this case, he'll appreciate any information that gets you both where you're trying to go.

Thinking the relationship is more meaningful if you've had sex. If you expect more from him than he's willing to give, you'll find yourself in trouble every time. Just because you're head's been shaken up by this one act doesn't mean his has. Chances are it hasn't.

Giving it up on the first date. First-date sex = casual. No judgments if you've given it up on the first date, but just know you'll have a damn hard time getting him to ever think of you as more than a hot hookup.

cheat SHEET

All right, ladies. A few reminders before we move along:

✓ Your intuition rarely fails you.

✓ Marriage isn't magic. It doesn't change people; it only magnifies who they are.

✓ When you ask a question, be prepared for every answer.

✓ When your partner has been dishonest with you, at least be honest with yourself.

✓ A liar is a cheater and a cheater is a liar. If you choose to stay, be realistic with your expectations.

chapter five

NO GOOD MAN
EVER THOUGHT
CRYING WAS CUTE

Remember when you were sixteen and you thought that all good romances came with a whole lotta crying and a heavy dose of drama? By the time I finished my first marriage, all I wanted was a Johnson's-baby-shampoo relationship—maybe not squeaky-clean, but at least one with no more tears. I cried a long time during those sixteen years of marriage, but I refused to be a long-suffering woman who gave up on a life of hot, buttery love.

Initially, I thought the problem between my husband and me was that we didn't know how to fight. I'd go back and forth in my head trying to work out what broke down between us when we disagreed. When I retraced the steps of nearly every fight we'd ever had, it seemed as though every argument came down to both of us desperately wanting to be heard and understood. Every time we got frustrated with one another, it was rarely about something we'd done—it was usually about what we *hadn't* done for each other.

When I figured out that learning how to fight right was really more about learning how to love right, moving forward in my next relationship felt a lot more like a romantic exploration than a tactical mission. Now I am able to approach our differences from a place of love rather than anger. My relationship with Jay is productive because we have both learned how to listen. When you stop trying to "win" an argument and start trying to understand why you're fighting in the first place, you minimize the time you have to wait to get to the makeup sex.

I know I talk a big game about how good Jay and I are at communicating—but that doesn't mean we always get it right. About six months into our marriage something came to a head that changed our relationship forever— and it was all for the better.

I've always been expressive with my love, and from the start of our relationship I'd tell Jay ten different ways from Sunday how I loved him, squealing things like

"Ooh, babe, I love you! You make me the happiest woman in the world!" and cooing, "Who's my favorite guy?" or "Hey, Mr. Wonderful!" into his ear when he got home. And he'd always be like, "Thanks, babe, that's nice," or, "I heard you the first time. How many times are you going to tell me that?" Finally, I broke down and asked, "That doesn't make your heart jump around? Don't you love me back?" I could tell right then that I'd lost him in the conversation, but we were onto something.

"Do you really question that?" Jay asked. "Didn't I just take off from work to fly all the way across the country so that you didn't have to go to that press event by yourself? Didn't I talk to every last person in that room, standing at your side before you even had the chance to ask? And you're going to ask me that? None of what I did registered?"

"Well, no, that was great that you did that. But you didn't say anything. You didn't say you loved me."

See, at the beginning of relationships, most people tend to give love in the way they want it reciprocated. But when you really love someone, your goal should be to give them what they need and trust that they will, in turn, give you what you need.

I'd already recognized what made Jay happy and what made him feel loved—doing things to show him I was taking care of him (the same kind of behavior he'd just described himself doing for me). So I started folding up all his laundry and leaving it on the bed for him to see rather than putting it away in his drawers, and that's when I'd hear:

"You did all that for me? Thank you, beautiful. Do you know how much I love you?"

"I *know* it, but I just want to actually hear you say it more. I'm showing you how to love me when I go on and on with the *I love you*s. I keep doing it because I'm trying to get you to give it back."

Finally, I was able to clearly tell my new husband that what Mama needs is ear candy, baby. Pour it on in there, and pour it on thick. You want these legs open, start at my ears.

At first Jay didn't get it: "I'm not a wordsmith. I'm not one of these guys that's going to tell you everything I'm feeling." And right then, the perfect teaching moment presented itself. I looked down the hall from our bedroom and saw my twelve-year-old daughter standing in the hall, forcing a pile of laundry taller than herself into the washing machine. "Pay attention to that," I said. "I'm not a domestic woman by nature. My daughter is a baby, and she does her own laundry. So every time I wash something for you? That is a labor of love and it costs me something. So if it costs you to tell me what I want to hear, pay the price, because I do it every day. It's real simple. It's not like I need Shakespeare; I just need to hear it often."

Finally, in my forties, I was having a conversation with my partner about how I wanted to be loved and asking him what being loved looked like to him. When we come to accept that the way we love and want to be loved differs from our partner's, we can then show each other that we were listening by making a concerted effort to meet one another's needs—everyone wins. Once I realized that what made Jay feel special was doing tasks for him that no one else in the world would think to do, I was able to spend more of my energy on that and less time giving him the lip service that was wasted on him. And when Jay realized that no matter how many nice chores he did for me, the most effective way of conveying his love for me was simple and steady verbal affirmations, he was able to make me feel better much more efficiently.

It's not rocket science, but once we have an open dialogue about what we want from someone else—when we remove the mystery and give the other person the answer key to the test of how to make us feel special, adored, valued, and revered—the chances of their passing with flying colors is almost 100 percent.

Conflict in any relationship is unavoidable, but when you care about someone, the goal of an argument isn't to win; it is to resolve. And compromise isn't about taking turns; it's about finding a middle ground. No healthy relationship should ever feel like a competition. You both got your trophy—each other! Now don't go and turn yourselves into each other's consolation prize. Go for the win-win!

SPEAK SOFTLY IF YOU WANT TO BE HEARD

$\mathscr{I}$ can recall, when I was younger, hearing my mother say those phrases, "Speak softly if you want to be heard," and, "There's a reason you have two ears and one mouth," listen twice as much as you speak, and latching onto both of them saved me many times growing up. Then, as I got older, I thought back to my childhood and all the times I heard my father yelling his head off at my mother, but I could never once remember hearing her voice through the bedroom wall.

I only learned later that it was because whenever she got upset, she would drop her voice into a low whisper. Though my father initially found the whole thing frustrating, I learned that eventually it made it difficult for him to have a screaming match with her because he'd have to lower his own voice just to hear what she was saying so that he could respond to it.

Even if you're not dealing with an especially argumentative person, it's still an important lesson to learn. When you show the other person that listening is just as important to you as being heard, you're acknowledging that his position gets as much value as yours, which means he's far more likely to respond in kind and give you equal time. He won't feel that the conversation is a power struggle for one party to be on top. I like to think of it as vocal mood lighting, bringing the tone down so that eventually you can get down.

When she says, "Whatever you want"—
She means "I sure hope you understand
what I want."

When he says, "Whatever you want"—
He means "Oh, hell, no, you aren't getting me to
screw this one up."

When she says, "I don't want to talk about it"—
She means "I really need to talk about it; I just don't
want to hear your opinion."

When he says, "I don't want to talk about it"—
He means "I really, really don't want to talk about it."

When she says, "Can we talk for a second"—
She means "Gotcha!"

THE ROAD TO RESOLUTION: ONE ALWAYS, TWO NEVERS, AND A SOMETIMES

*B*ecause healthy communication is about understanding your partner as well as you know yourself, and every couple's path toward understanding is different, I'm not always a fan of absolutes. But once you've done all of the work that you can to understand whom you're dealing with, you should file four surefire strategies under *Use to Defuse*. Bust them out when conflict arises. You can thank me later!

1. ALWAYS FIND SOMETHING TO APOLOGIZE FOR

I have a friend who never apologizes for anything. She'd die from starvation if it took an "I'm sorry" to get her the last morsel of food on earth. And that's how I used to be—until I realized that if I wanted closeness with anyone, it was more important to restore my relationship with the person than it was to be right. Being alone with your rightness doesn't feel anywhere near as good as sharing a home with someone you love.

In the heat of an argument, I'm not saying it's necessary to take total responsibility for something that's no fault of your own. But simply demonstrating that you're aware and that you appreciate that your partner has an opinion different from yours goes a long way. Try for something like "I'm sorry it took me this long to figure out you feel this way," instead of just "I'm sorry you feel that way." It's as simple as that. Appreciating that your partner's feelings are just as valid as yours rather than laying blame or getting defensive about your role shows him that you respect his feelings and want to make things right between you.

2. NEVER TELL SOMEONE HOW TO FEEL

So often people don't understand that feelings and logic are two unrelated things, and just because you don't understand why a person feels a particular way doesn't mean that the person's feelings are any less real or important. You can't tell someone that he or she shouldn't feel hurt. It's not up to you to decide whether your partner feels wronged. It's not up to you to decide how someone feels about anything. Listen to the feelings your partner has and try to find a considerate response to them. You can't control how your partner reacts to a situation; you can only respond to your partner's feelings with love and a desire to make both of you come out of it positively.

3. NEVER ISSUE THREATS OR ULTIMATUMS

You haven't kidnapped his child. You aren't trying to frame him for murder. You're just trying to get him to understand what's bothering you. When you introduce additional stakes to win or lose your argument, you're just falsely inflating the direness of the situation, and you only make the problem you're trying to fix that much bigger. Talk directly to the issue you have and work toward a mutually agreed-upon solution. People always respond better to open dialogue than to demands. Instead of "If you want to go to the game with your friends instead of picking up our daughter from that birthday party, you aren't getting any action from me this weekend," try "Baby, I know you'd intended to go to the game this weekend, but if you'd make time just this once to do me a solid and pick up our baby girl at four, the rest of the night is yours to do with what you please."

4. SOMETIMES IT'S EASIER TO TAKE OFF YOUR TOP THAN TO THROW IN THE TOWEL

When all other resolution angles have failed you, it may be time to break out the big guns to calm the beast. I like to excuse myself for a moment when things have gotten especially tense and come back in little bitty boy shorts, a wife-beater, and no bra, with my hair in a ponytail and my face scrubbed clean. To my husband, I look raw and vulnerable, and it also looks as if I could get naked at any moment, which means that all bets—and arguments, and clothes—are off, too. No one caves, no one takes the blame, but the fighting's done. Because, as he knows better than anyone else—it's hard to fight naked!

DON'T FORGET THE MAKEUP SEX—EVER!

*E*ven if you're able to defuse the situation without resorting to your feminine wiles, the best part of any fight is getting naked and getting busy afterward. I don't care how tired you are; it doesn't matter if you're secretly not entirely satisfied with how things shook out in the fight, or if you'd rather be watching the finale of *So You Think You Can Dance*— when the fight is over, your night has only just begun. You must sign this peace treaty with more than a kiss. If you need to excuse yourself to splash water on your face, take care of yourself first, but just remember that all the passion you both just built up for this moment needs to be translated into positive, sexual energy as soon as possible. Don't hug it out. Don't schedule it for later. Get down on it—now, girl!

DEFUSE AND CONQUER

Couples usually fight about one of three things. The good news? You only have three things to worry about!

Sex. You won't always want it at the same time. Accept that and move on. In my experience, it takes up less time and anguish to have sex when you don't want it than it does to fight about how little sex you have.

Money. Every couple needs one clear chief financial officer, and this isn't a male or female thing. It's a "whoever got the A in algebra thing." Make a choice about who is the bookkeeper and respect that this person has both of your interests at heart.

The past. Once you've moved beyond old issues and forgiven the past, it's time to leave it there. Forgiveness is accepting that what's happened can't be undone and trusting that it won't be repeated. And when it comes to social media, wouldn't you rather "defriend" an old flame than "unboyfriend" the most important man in your life?

CONFRONT WITH THE TRUTH, AFFIRM WITH LOVE

Sometimes in a relationship we fall into behavior patterns that aren't healthy. We don't always see it coming, and it's not always clear to both parties that someone is suffering. Not everyone is a fan of confrontation, but it doesn't need to feel like an attack when you are constructive in your approach. I know it sounds like a bunch of mumbo jumbo, but if you're able to express your relationship concerns with an equal level of appreciation for the things in your relationship that are working, your grievances will feel less like points of contention and more like an honest inquiry into how the two of you could make your relationship stronger.

Several years ago, *affirmation* became a big buzzword in the spiritual community—we were all supposed to find pathways and people that would validate our feelings and make us feel good about the emotions we had. It always made sense to me on a practical level, but I didn't ever see its productive powers in practice until a friend of mine explained how an honest confrontation coupled with loving affirmation made her marriage stronger than ever.

When she first met her husband, his domineering mother soon came into the picture. At first she found it funny, cute even, how her boyfriend always deferred to his mother and leapt to her side whenever she so much as lost the remote control. Eventually, though, my friend started feeling that she was playing second fiddle to her soon-to-be mother-in-law and felt that three was a crowd. He always took his mother's side in arguments— even when she went on the offensive against his fiancée. Still, my friend married him, but she eventually felt that his codependency with his mother was eating away at the core of the marriage—a silent undermining neither of them would ever address.

Fortunately, my friend was able to sort through her

feelings and recognize that so many of his wonderful qualities were what created the problem in the first place, and if he and she were able to recalibrate them, everyone would be much happier. She could tell that he knew something was wrong, but she also knew he was struggling to come up with a solution that wouldn't hurt anyone.

One night not long after the holidays, she calmly sat him down after dinner. "Baby, I can't tell you how respectable it is to see how much attention and respect you are so careful to give your mother, and I can't tell you how important it is to me that you'll be able to show our children how to properly treat a woman. And I know it must be hard for her to share a man as wonderful as you with me. Please hear me when I say that I don't want you to ever disrespect her in any way, but now that you have two women in your life who want the best for you—we also expect the best from you, which sometimes means you're going to have to work twice as hard.

"The upshot for you is that you have love and support coming in from all directions. And as challenging as I know it will be for you, I need to feel like my needs are being met as your wife. I don't doubt that you can do it—I married you for the capacity to love that I saw in your heart. I just think we need to talk about this now before I begin resenting her or you."

Her husband's eyes welled up with tears. Apparently this wasn't the first time his relationship with his mother had caused problems—but it was the first time any of his partners had ever validated him for being a good son to her. And what he loved even more? That instead of expecting him to be capable of mind reading, his wife had the confidence in their relationship and herself to come to him with her concerns long before the issue turned into something that would plague their relationship for years to come. Since then, both she and her mother-in-law have also recognized the importance of supporting each other. Using honesty rather than guilt gets the job done much quicker. Everyone involved feels that their needs are being addressed when you take time out to discuss how you're trying to achieve that.

MAINTAINING MARITAL BLISS

If you're preparing to head down the aisle with the man of your dreams, it's likely that you and your betrothed have hit some bumps in the road as you learned how to love each other. And as wonderful as your wedding day will be, getting hitched rarely comes off without a hitch. With big checks flying and familial obligations weighing heavily, it's important to cut off foreseeable complications at the pass before they mess with your big day.

Keep in-laws out of the planning. Chances are you're still getting to know your fiancé's parents, not to mention the dynamic they have with their son. People get emotional about the strangest things surrounding a wedding, and you don't want to accidentally walk into a minefield. Though everybody's mama needs to feel that she's being heard, make most major decisions with your mate alone, so you can present them to both sets of parents with a united front.

Sort out which small stuff is yours to sweat. If he can't tell the difference between a peony and a pansy, he probably shouldn't be too involved in the bouquet business, but if he

usually handles deejay duties at home, leave the song selection up to him. With so many tasks to divvy up, it's a good idea to set up a plan of how best to divide and conquer.

Keep your expectations realistic. Not everyone is comfortable being in the spotlight, and neither of you should pretend to be someone you are not on your wedding day. Unless both of you want to write your own vows, it's best to leave those up to the professionals. And only make that first dance as long as is comfortable for both of you.

Let him have one last run with his boys. You may not like his old roommate, and after today you don't have to pretend to. But you should probably give your man one last chance to recognize the friends who helped him become the man he is today. Chances are he wouldn't choose to be trapped on a desert island with some of your bridesmaids either.

Throw him a bone when it comes to the registry. If you're handling most of the details yourself but you don't want him to feel left out, let him go a little nuts picking out items for the registry. If you end up getting anything truly tacky, you can always return it!

cheqt **SHEET**

Learn to fight right! Here's your crib sheet for keeping calm when conflicts arise.

✓ Most arguments can be traced back to that moment when one of you thought you weren't being heard. Address that moment—not the one you're fighting about now.

✓ The goal of an argument with a loved one isn't to win; it's to resolve.

✓ You can always find one thing to apologize for.

✓ Keep your eyes on the prize—makeup sex!

chapter six

WHO SAID LOVE
IS UNCONDITIONAL?

know that I talk a lot about being a romantic, but at this point in our relationship, I'm pretty sure you have a clear picture of how practically I view this not-so-crazy little thing called love. I'm under no faulty notion that love is something delivered by chubby babies with bows and arrows. That's why I always tell my husband, "I love you today." He ignored it initially, then started laughing it off, but after he kept hearing it, he finally asked, "Why do you say 'today'? Are you not going to love me tomorrow?"

I replied, "I don't know. Am I?" Jay looked at me, confused, so I explained, "The bottom line is this: my love is not unconditional. You can't come in here, talk crazy to me, hurt my feelings, run over my emotions, and still think I'm gonna feel the same way about you. I'm not. So, I'm gonna tell you how I feel today based on how you behave. You might not be the same person tomorrow. But today, brother, you're all right. And I have every reason to believe you will be tomorrow, too. But it all depends on you staying true to the man I love and married, and me staying true to myself."

So, no, my love is not unconditional, and I don't expect that from my partner either. I believe that when you get married, you make a vow to fulfill your commitment to the person standing in front of you that very day. But if the terms of the agreement change—if you or your mate changes your core values, if either of you has failed to disclose pertinent details—the contract's null and void. I don't mean to say that people can't change; I just mean that we sometimes need to review the contract before we re-up for another year. And that's okay! We're all constantly evolving. And in a loving relationship, hopefully you're doing so together so that the enterprise is even greater than the one you envisioned the day you vowed to be together. I'm on my second husband now because things changed—and I'm the happier for it; I'm sure my first husband is, too.

Have you ever had that moment in a relationship when you look over at your mate in the middle of the night and think, *Who are you and how did you get up in here?* Maybe his priorities have shifted from being a committed boyfriend to becoming a laser-focused businessman, or maybe he's begun displaying behaviors that no longer allow you to love him as freely as you once did—disrespecting your family, drinking too much, caring more about himself than you, lying about how he spends his time. While we have to trust in our choices, not everything is revealed about a person when you fall in love with him or her, and you often learn a lot about a person during the tough times—which don't usually happen until you're in pretty deep. That's why before you get to the crossroads moments of your life together, you need to be as well-informed as you can about how he responds when the chips are down.

He may love you today, but how's he going to be when your mama gets sick? Is he a strong enough man to work through your difficulty getting pregnant? Will he be able to handle it if he gets laid off for six months and you become the breadwinner? You can't actually know how he'll respond to any of these situations until they arrive, and you need to accept that your view of him may change when they do. Love is a big step to take—but don't go thinking it's one you can't take back!

LOVE IS A CHOICE, NOT A CONDITION

$\mathscr{I}$ don't know when this whole idea of "falling in love" started, but love is something to fully stand up in and walk through consciously. For women who talk about some smacked-over-the-head-with-a-frying-pan kind of love, I'm here to tell you that being in love is a decision that you make; it is not something that just *happens* to you.

Let me say it again: love is a choice you make of your own free will, and that freedom of choice is the most beautiful gift God gave us. Yet so many people talk about love as if it were some sort of force that overtakes you. I believe you can be attracted to someone, you can be infatuated with someone, you can want nothing more than to be on your back with your knees pinned behind your ears with someone, but don't go confusing lust for love.

You may not be able to help whom you are attracted to, but you *can* choose whom you love and how. And that is to say that love is a commitment your heart *and* your mind make. It is an active and ever-evolving process, a conscious choice that takes effort and maintenance. Infatuation is the easy part, which lesser-evolved animals do every day with a different partner. The hard part is taking the feelings of lust, evaluating whether you can turn those feelings into a productive relationship, and translating it into the life you want for yourself. Make sense?

First, take a look at how your man treats you and how he makes you feel—that should always be your first consideration. Next, consider why his past relationships ended and what kind of friends he runs around with—this is important to know if you're looking to build a life with this man. Then ask yourself whether you could picture a life beyond sex with him. If all of these signs are positive, only then should you give yourself permission to love him. Be honest with yourself—don't go telling yourself you're in the love with the man he could be; you gotta love the man standing in front of you right now. Otherwise, he will always disappoint you. And whose fault is that?

Because I recognize that being in love is a choice—that it's something I have control over—I am never afraid to tell a man I love him before he says he loves me. I never want to be in a relationship with anyone who makes me feel as if I need to be guarded, that I can't say what I think or how I feel. I certainly don't want to date a liar, so I don't expect to hear the same sentiment back right away. I'm comfortable enough to know that people "fall" when they "fall."

When I told Jay I loved him, he looked like a deer caught in headlights, and I had to cut him off before his mouth started running faster than his brain. "I'm not telling you that so you can tell me back," I said. "I'm just telling you because that's how I feel. But my truth is not predicated on yours being the same. My truth is that I love you, and that's it. Now, let's move on. What're we doing for dinner?"

He was panicked, waiting for the other shoe to drop, but he needn't have worried. I was honest with him about how I felt, and I was totally fine that he went for a month without telling me that he loved me back because I didn't want to hear it unless he meant it. Sometimes you just give to give, and you trust that when your hand is open to give, it's also open to receive. There's nothing wrong with deciding you're in love with someone before he loves you. You just need to know yourself well enough to recognize if you are telling him because you expect him to say in return he loves you, or if you just want him to know how you feel and are prepared to wait and see if he develops the same feelings for you.

The worst thing you can do is to say "I love you" with the expectation of hearing it back. If you fall apart because your feelings aren't immediately reciprocated, don't bother saying anything at all until you are confident enough in your love that you can tell your man about it without hesitation and without expecting to hear it back right away. (Oh, and if you call it "the L-word" as if it were a four-letter word, you're not ready.)

Telling one another you love each other for the first time is not some kind of power struggle or game of chicken. When you have conviction in your feelings and express them out of love, you never have to worry about seeming needy because you have chosen love; it's not some helpless, irrational condition you've found your-self in.

When Jay finally did tell me he loved me, it was over the phone while I was on set shooting late one night.

"Hey, Niecy. I want to come see you."

"Okay, I'll be here. I love you. See you soon."

"I love you, too."

"Well, it's about time."

I was half-joking when I said that. This simple conversation was made so much sweeter because I knew that he meant it. By the time he got there, I knew I really had my man, and he had me, and we were on an equal footing. Neither of us was forcing anything in the relationship; we came to love each other organically and honestly.

lost in TRANSLATION

When he says, "I don't want to talk about it anymore, babe"—
He means "I need to get my thoughts together. I don't want to argue, I just don't know what to say."

When she says, "I'm not sure I can do this anymore"—
She means "This is your Hail Mary. Please give me some reasons to stay."

When he says, "How about we go for a ride, just you and me?"—
He means "I miss you. I miss us."

When she says, "How about we go to a movie, just you and me?"—
She means "You don't get to pick what we're seeing."

When he says, "My friends are having a party, we should go."— He means "I like what's happening with us and I want to show you off."

I WAS BORN TO BE *A* WIFE— NOT NECESSARILY *YOUR* WIFE

About three months before I married Jay, I realized it was time we had yet another heart-to-heart before we took the plunge in front of all our friends, family, and an entire camera crew filming a two-hour special for TLC. So I said, "I want to let you know that if you feel like you're having cold feet and want to back out of this, now is the time to say so and I will walk away with no hard feelings. But if you're questioning this, you need to tell me while we can still get off the ride."

He looked a little stunned, maybe even a bit hurt, but I needed him to understand that I was committing to marriage and I needed to make sure he understood me. So I explained, "I'm looking pretty good right now. I've lost all this weight for our big day, my skin has never looked better, I've been doing every crazy treatment imaginable to prepare for the wedding. Still, if you were to tell me today that you didn't want to go through with it, I would let you go. Just know that the next time we run into each other, the first words out of my mouth would be "This is my new husband. This is the man who you let come up in here and steal your good thing."

I realized I still wasn't being entirely clear, so I told him that what I meant was that I wanted to give him the opportunity to change his mind, because I'd done this before. The first time around I'd been so consumed with all the trappings of getting married and wanting to be married, that it wasn't until I had a mortgage, a baby, and some extra stretch marks that I took a step back and really examined what I was doing. At forty-five, Jay had never entered into anything like this, and I wanted him to know it was okay if he needed a moment to recognize that he wasn't just committing to me—he was committing to the idea of marriage altogether.

Jay considered my words, then said, "I know you say you're a person who wants to get married, but is it just that you want to get married, or do you want to marry me?"

"Both. See, I am a wife, and that's what I know for sure. I don't know whether or not you're a husband—only you know that. So even if I don't marry you, honey, I'm still going to marry somebody, because that's my truth. I tasted being single and I'm not built for it. I don't want to go to the club. I don't want to wear Spanx every day. I don't want to stay on top of a bunch of different guys. I just want to get up underneath one. You might not be built for that, and I can't be mad at you for who you are, but tell me before we say, 'I do.' I love you, and I want to marry you, which is why I'm being completely honest with you."

My priority in a relationship is honesty, and my preference is being married—I needed to be sure Jay understood that before we got hitched. He appreciated my honesty because he knew it was coming from a place of love and not intended to be negative or hurtful. Ever since then, whenever any question comes up—how do you feel about this, that, the third and the thunderbird—we've always been able to share the unvarnished truth.

The foundation of our marriage was built on solid

ground, with all our cards and expectations laid out on the table. We left no room for unrealistic notions about love that would leave us feeling let down in the future. If you want your needs to be met, you have to tell your man what they are in no uncertain terms. Lord knows, if you sit around waiting for him to figure it out on his own, you'll be waiting a long time.

PROVIDING THE PROVISION
FOR THE VISION

*N*ow, once you've chosen love, how do you go about keeping this good thing going? One of the most important factors in sustaining a relationship is to never fall out of love with each other at the same time. That may sound simple, but trust me, it is easier said than done.

For starters, we need to feed our partners a steady diet of support and encouragement, reassuring them that we share their goals and applauding their commitment to actualizing their dreams, *and* we expect the same treatment in return. Does he want to start his own business? Does he hope to become a partner in his law firm so that he can provide financially for his family in ways far greater than anything he grew up with? Do you want to be a stay-at-home mom because you want to be the chief caregiver for your children? If you enter into a relationship knowing these things, you do so with the understanding that certain sacrifices have to be made. The key is to understand what his and your goals are for the relationship you're creating. You can't be surprised when he's putting in late hours while you're waiting on him to come home. He can't resent that you don't have career ambitions if from the get-go you told him you didn't want to be away from your children while they were young.

To be someone's partner means that their interests and your interests are the same—that one's profit is the other's gain. If these interests or goals begin to oppose one another, the partnership will eventually become unsustainable. But if you enter into a partnership with full disclosure of all your liabilities as well as a clear game plan of where you want to take the newly formed union, then what strengthens him should also strengthen you and vice versa.

The chief source of capital that you provide one another is loving support and encouragement. A lot of men miss the boat when it comes to understanding what emotional care looks like. So don't hesitate to spell it out! At the beginning, you might need to give him plenty of concrete examples of what feeling loved means to you. As I said before, men tend to speak in headlines, while we women like to get on down to the fine print. But, be sure to ask what feeling loved means to him, too. Then, it's both of your jobs (and I do mean *jobs*) to keep the love coming in many different forms.

THE CHECKS AND BALANCES
OF A SUCCESSFUL PARTNERSHIP

*B*oth of you need to be tenacious in protecting the stability of your relationship. When you're both committed to maintaining the highest performance standards, you raise each other's game to the next level. It may not sound sexy in those terms, but it is what it is.

1. KEEP UP THE WOOING

Woo early and often and never let up—this goes for both of you. Remember how excited you were the first time he said, "I can't stop thinking about you." Well, he liked hearing that, too! We all want to feel considered, and if we try to behave in ways that show we're still out to impress, surprise, and excite one another the way we did when we first started dating, the message is clear.

Finding ways to show your appreciation for your mate is paramount for having a balanced and lasting relationship. For me, the clearest demonstration that my husband recognizes my needs and wants to fulfill them is—wait for it—chores! If I don't have to ask him to catch that corner of the bed when he sees me making it up, or if I remember the brand of detergent he preferred before we moved in together, it's like a little pinch in the ass that says, "I know you, babe."

When it comes to mealtime (particularly if you and your spouse both work full-time), it's important that neither of you feels as if you've done *all* the work to get dinner on the table. Equal division of labor is important in maintaining balance in your relationship. If one of you feels beleaguered and underappreciated in the kitchen, that feeling will likely carry over into the bedroom later on that night—and if you do try to have sex, it's only going to feel like one more task for the worker bee to bang out, which won't be fun for everyone. In a perfect world, you can negotiate who's doing what when it comes to preparing the meal based on everyone's needs, and then you can share dishes *and* some kisses in the kitchen when you're done.

Jay and I have a custom of taking each other on mystery dates, too. He'll call up to say that the children are taken care of, give me an idea of what to wear and when he'll pick me up, and leave the rest a surprise. I still get excited every time, wondering where he's going to take me, just as I did when we were in that first phase of getting to know one another.

My girlfriend Tracy and her husband like to recall the Jamaican honeymoon they took, and while they can't fly to the Caribbean twelve times a year, they do make a habit of going out for jerk chicken pretty regularly. When you keep memories of your early love alive, it keeps your relationship as fresh as it was when you loved your partner for the first time.

2. KEEP A COMMON INTEREST

If the only thing you and your husband share anymore is a mortgage payment and the urge to dodge calls from each other's mama, you're in trouble. Rather than faking it through a Giants game or dragging him to an art museum he doesn't even want to pay the price of parking to visit, pick a new hobby you can share just with one another. Jay and I decided to take up cycling, and the day we bought those bikes, we rode them straight into the bedroom. Now every time we hop on those things, it's just another form of foreplay.

3. KEEP IT TIGHT

Just because you got the ring does not mean you can skimp on your beauty routine. I'm not saying you need to look like his bride for the next forty years of his life, but we all know it only takes a minimal effort to get him off the streets and into the sheets—so it's important to keep yourself together to show him that you care that he's attracted to you.

But, ladies, let's be honest. All the primping and prep work—it's more for you than it is for your man. If men need to feel that you're spending all that time and money at the beauty salon or at the gym to make them feel good, then let them think it. But we all know we feel better about ourselves and we feel sexier when we've spent some time pampering ourselves.

It's not about dropping a down payment's worth of cash at a spa, either. It's about taking time for yourself and taking care of yourself. When you aren't just going through the motions the way you do in the morning, or rushing your ass through some special treatments to look your best before a wedding, you can take the time to make the ritual all about you, on your own time, and on your own terms.

On a night when you know your man is going to be out, grab a bottle of white wine and a candle or two and lock yourself in the bathroom for a night of beauty. Soak in the tub and lather on that mask you've always meant to apply. (This may require a straw for your wine!) Paint your nails a color you've been scared to go for. If you're one of those women who still have their own hair, God bless you, tonight is the night to leave that V05 hot-oil treatment in for forty-five minutes. There is no rushing through a night of self-care.

By the time he gets home, you'll be refreshed and rejuvenated, he'll get the feeling that his lady still knows how to take care of herself, and if you've managed to keep yourself away from the nozzle, you could have a long night of sweet-smelling lovemaking ahead of you—so keep the candles on!

PRESERVE THE MYSTIQUE

Childbirth doesn't have to mean the death of your sex life, but going from fizzle to sizzle takes work. You can't control that baby's crying, but you sure can make him wanna keep trying.

1. Keep him on the north side of the sheet during the delivery. His thoughts of this area of your body should always be sexy and never messy. Preserve the mystique!

2. Keep the kids out of your bed. "What God has brought together let no screaming baby put asunder." The Book of Niecy. You never know when you'll have a free moment to get down, so always stay ready!

3. Wear something that makes you feel sexy. Boy shorts, thigh-high stockings, silk anything—whatever works for you to work it!

4. Celebrate your jiggly parts. Act like you like 'em if you want someone else to!

4. KEEP SWITCHING IT UP

The only thing better than sex is new sex. It ain't chocolate or any other lies that polite or delusional people may tell you; it's new sex. And since you gotta keep this marriage going till they throw dirt on your coffin, it's important to constantly introduce new moves in the sack and have some tricks up your sleeve to rotate into your lovemaking, doling it out in small doses, and leaving a little sauce for the ribs.

At the beginning, of course, it's going to be tricky. You want to be sure it's clear you know your way around the bedroom without looking as if you were a professional—unless he's into that sort of thing—don't judge! (Does your man like strip clubs? Throw your soul on a pole and enjoy! I bought an amazing retractable one for our bedroom.)

It's also about keeping current, and by that I don't mean picking up a *Cosmo* every once in a while and staying on top of your Kegel exercises. I mean being up-to-date on the latest sex techniques from experts as well as remaining aware of how your sexual chemistry is evolving with your partner. Technique books and online forums are a great source for moves you've never considered. When you become aware of the many directions your sex life can go and you discover which paths bring you the most satisfaction, use these resources as a choose-your-own-sex-adventure guide!

5. KEEP THE PARTY GOING

In our house, Jay and I love to celebrate anything and everything, so no event is too small to bust out chocolate and champagne. We observe all of our firsts—the first time we met, our first date, the first time he saw me naked, the first time he helped me take out my weave. . . . We throw a party for just about everything except for the first time I met his mama. That didn't go as well as it could have.

Making milestones out of molehills turns every little thing you've experienced into another reason to toast your love, and there ain't nothing wrong with that. (It always leads to a pretty sexy after-party, too.)

WHEN IT'S ALL OVER BUT THE SHOUTIN', WHY NOT SKIP THE SHOUTIN'?

My mother told me when I divorced my first husband, "You will have the peace to leave when you know you've done all you can to try to make it work. If there's anything you haven't done, do it." And I tell people all the time, "If you're gonna be in the same house, you might as well work on it."

You have to try everything before you walk away. That way you won't have regret. "Damn, if we just would have went to counseling. . . . If only I'd started eating dinner with my family more often, maybe things would have changed for the better." But once you've tried all that you possibly can, you need to be honest with yourself about what you want and the reality of how your current situation can or cannot meet those needs and desires.

We've spent a lot of time here on ways of keeping a relationship thriving, but not everyone is worth keeping, and that's okay, too. We can all be such victims of stinkin' thinkin'—trapped by the idea that you have to do things a certain way—and that includes being devastated by every breakup we have.

A few years ago, I broke up with a guy right at New Year's Eve. The next day I was wailing and gnashing and crying and saying I couldn't eat. So my girlfriends came over, put a damp, cold towel on my head, champagne in an IV drip, and everybody was rubbing my back, giving me the speech about how I was better than him and that he didn't deserve me. While I was crying in bed, my friends were hovering around me like little cackling hens. And while they were well-intentioned, it was doing *nothing* constructive to make me feel better.

Then it dawned on me as I was lying there: *I left this situation because it wasn't right. Why am I grieving that? If this is really not God's best for me, why am I crying because*

He revealed it? So I bolted up and said, "Get off of me, all y'all. Get off of me!"

I had to be honest with myself. I knew he wasn't the best for me. And so many times we break up with someone and believe that we are supposed to mourn the loss, but the truth is, if you know that man isn't the best you can do, then that means your best is yet to come. And that should be a good feeling—knowing that your life has the potential to get much better.

As soon as I had that epiphany, I grabbed the phone and called the guy: "Listen, we broke up. We both know it wasn't working. Why don't we have the best breakup in the history of the world? Instead of having these sad conversations where you can tell over the phone I'm crying, and then I show up with your sweatshirt on and a box of your stuff, and then I have to take the sweatshirt off and have on the world's tiniest tank top to see if that makes you want me back—before we do all that, why don't we just agree to celebrate the good things that we brought to each other and give each other permission to go find what is best for both of us?"

He waited for the catch but there was none. I asked him, "Do you want to break up in Hawaii? Let's just go to Hawaii and break up there." So we went to Hawaii, we surfed, we ate shrimp, we ran around and had a great time, and on day four, I dropped his ass off at the airport, and I haven't seen him since.

So many people were like, "Oh, my God, weren't you scared y'all were going to get back together?" I wasn't because I was honest with myself that it wasn't for me. And in doing so, the healing was quicker. Rather than wasting time going out with friends, talking about how I just got out of something and I wasn't ready to date, I found it easier to say, "You taught me a lot about family. You taught me a lot about what it means to put your kids first. When it came to Hollywood, you showed me things I'd never done before. You know you're still crazy when it comes to x, y, and z, but I appreciate you for these things. I hope you have a great life and get the things you want out of it." Two to the chest, peace sign, and scramola—the exit was fantastic. Which made my entrance into my next relationship so much better.

When I walked out of that situation, I didn't pull on my bathrobe extratight and grab a pint of Häagen-Dazs. No! I sashayed outta there like, "All right, bring on the men!" I was ready. And sure enough, my Jay wasn't far away.

 **REVAMP**

RESTORING QUALITY TIME

Maintaining intimacy is an incredibly challenging part of any relationship. Work, kids, complacency—all these things can conspire to distance partners from one another. Now's not the time to let the wheels fall off—remind each other often why you're worth it. Make time for sex—it doesn't always have to be an all-night affair.

Remember the importance of touch. There's a difference between PDAs and sweet reminders that you love one another. When you walk past him in the kitchen, take the opportunity to rub your hand along his back. When talking to him during the game, why not make your point by touching his leg occasionally? It's not about groping—it's about giving your man constant affirmations that he is loved.

Steal some secret one-on-one time. For me and Jay, it's as simple as sitting in the car together for five minutes, just us. It's fun to feel as if we're sneaking away at the end of the workday, before it's time to help out with the kids' homework, cook dinner, or check out in front of the TV. Sometimes we don't even

talk—mmhmm!—mostly it's about having a quick connection in the middle of the chaos that our life often is.

Use technology to bring you closer together, not push you farther apart. Instead of only texting your man a list of things to pick up at the store, why not send him a sexy text in the middle of the day? And if you *really* want to show him you care, get on Skype—I may be stuck on set all day, but that doesn't mean I can't spare a few minutes in my dressing room to get intimate with my man over the Internet. Find some time—and some privacy—and get to spreading the love.

cheat SHEET

Remember—your love is here to stay. Until it isn't. Here are some quick hits on when to stay and when to go.

- ✓ Love is a choice; it's not something you fall uncontrollably into.

- ✓ A committed relationship should be a mutually beneficial partnership. Work to ensure the two of you have your interests aligned, and constantly work to maintain and tenaciously protect them.

- ✓ If the terms of your agreement change, the contract may be voided at any time.

- ✓ Never forget that you are meant to be loved by someone. Everyone deserves it.

conclusion

You're still here? That's my girl—way to hang in there. . . . This means you're armed with all the best information about yourself and ready to get out there to find and receive the best the world is ready to give you!

I know I can go on and on and *on* when it comes to love. But that's because I believe finding love and holding on to it is so much simpler than we make it out to be. Most important, I believe that we each deserve to have love, to share love, and to receive love.

Now, I know it must be frustrating for some of you to hear a married woman tell you that love is simple if you're feeling that it's the last thing in the cards for you right now. But keep in mind that I said it was simple; I never said it was easy—which is an important distinction to make. If love were easy to find, and easy to maintain, it wouldn't be worth it. Nothing worthwhile ever is.

So it's important to remind yourself that it's not only okay, but completely understandable, if you haven't found love yet. I just hope that I've given you some useful tools to help you demystify it—figuring out how you love and how you want to be loved in return will help you find whom you love. I don't know about you, but I'm ready for you to find love. However, mastering the formula isn't the hard part. Doing the required homework on yourself and sticking to a plan? That's when it gets tricky.

It can be so easy to psych yourself out, put on that playlist of sad songs, and eat ice cream all night—which can actually be a fine way to spend an evening every now and again, but it ain't the way to go through life . . . especially when your future partner is out there, completely within your reach.

So many people talk about being in a relationship as if it were a game, as if there were some kind of bag of tricks women need to ensnare a man—or some crazy mind tricks to use on him so that he conforms to expectations, whether they're realistic or not. I want to debunk the idea that any of this is as complicated as it's made out to be. When it comes to love, there are no rules to play by, no rules to break, nor is it some kind of sport—some version of "Two can play at that game!" If anything, healthy relationships are an art form, not child's play.

Who would want to play a game for the rest of their lives? That's not being real; that's not being truthful—that goes against everything I've tried to impart here about being true to yourself. The most important lessons to take away from this book apply to both men and women. Here is your cheat sheet to finding love through openness, positivity, and practicality:

1. Walk in your truth. Behave in a way that reflects your best self and doesn't compromise what you hold dear, not in the way you feel someone else might appreciate you more.

2. Know the man you want. Ask yourself who your ideal partner is and what love from him looks like. Make sure you want him for reasons that get you the maximum benefit. Prioritize.

3. Ask for him. Be clear about what you want and don't waste time on people who don't have the same goals in life and love.

4. Be patient. Recognize that love won't always come exactly when you want it, but like God, it's always on time.

At the core, I think that changing your circumstances has everything to do with your thoughts. If you believe a certain thing hard enough and long enough, then you can create your own reality. When all my girlfriends were saying that men were dogs who would always let me down, I refused to listen. I told them I didn't believe that every man was going to disappoint me; even though I think a great number of men cheat, I still believed I could be one of the lucky ones who didn't get lied to.

The man I asked the universe for didn't show up the next day; it wasn't as if I'd rubbed a magic lamp and the genie granted me my wish. But eventually my guy showed up—and all the time I put in, working toward being ready to receive a man who was a reflection of me feels like a small price to have paid compared to the lifetime of love I have ahead of me.

Just last year I heard about an old couple in their nineties who wound up in the hospital together after getting into a car accident. They'd been married for seventy-two years, and they asked that their beds be placed close enough together so that they could hold hands. Eventually things got bad and the doctors could tell that the man had stopped breathing—for several minutes. But they couldn't figure out why his heart monitor was still registering a heartbeat. Then they figured out that the woman's heartbeat was being transferred through her hand into his, and it was beating for both of them. This was not some Hallmark Channel movie—it was real! The woman's heart beat for both of them until the very end. That's the kind of love I'm working for every day with Jay—and so far, so good!

So when something in my life is broken, I take it back to the manufacturer. For me, that's God. It may not be for you, and that's okay. My owner's manual is the Bible. At times in my life when I've felt broken, I've read it and it told me, "Love is patient. Love is kind. It does not boast of itself. It never fails. It hopes all things. It believes all things."

I'm, like, *Oh, okay, so I got the instruction*. I know that love is what we were created for, and I work toward putting it out in the world every day, in everything I do, because I believe we owe it to one another.

And you know what other Bible passage I love? In Genesis, where it says that before sin, Adam and Eve were naked in the Garden of Eden and they were not ashamed. (I imagine most of the fighting only started after they started stitching together bush-leaf bikini bottoms.) If they'd only stayed naked with one another—literally and figuratively—things would have ended so much better for them and for us.

And so I encourage you: be naked as much as possible, especially when you're fighting! The results will amaze you!

Love, Niecy

epilogue: jay weighs in

BY JAY TUCKER

Make no mistake, I'm not trying to get the last word in here. Niecy just thought you might want to hear a little bit from her husband after hearing so much *about* her husband. When we started throwing our match-maker parties after we were dating and in love, it was because we *both* wanted to make this whole process easier for our friends. Though I don't have nearly the following my wife does, when it comes to dating advice, thanks to finding and holding a woman as special as she is, I get plenty of questions from guys I know about how to navi-gate the dating-and-relationship world better.

I agree with absolutely everything that my wife has written in this book . . . and it's not just because she's read-ing this over my shoulder as I type. It's just that we see it all similarly—Niecy often says that I'm the male version of her. We feel strongly about all the big-ticket issues, and it all starts with the most important element to any healthy relationship: honesty. Which is why I'm going to throw down some truths for both men and women here. Hopefully it will help you find a love as abiding as the one Niecy and I work toward preserving every single day.

FOR THE GUYS

$\mathcal{I}$ was more than ready to be in a committed relationship when I met Niecy. I'd lived a full life as a bachelor—the details of which I will not give, because I want to remain happily married! However, I will say that whether I was in a relationship or seeing someone casually, I was always honest about my intentions and expectations.

This is the same advice I give to my guy friends: Be honest with the ladies that you are dating or sleeping with. Give them the option to make an informed decision. Don't be afraid to tell her if you are interested in her but still interested in dating other women. You may be surprised with the response. Women will respect your honesty. It is on *every* woman's priority list. Don't feel pressured to lie or deceive because you're worried about telling her something you think she won't want to hear. There is always someone who wants to play ball the way you do.

When we men play the field, we must do so with integrity. The golden rule for all men when it comes to women: treat them as you would have another man treat your mother or sister or daughter—it's as simple as that. Otherwise we contribute to the growing list of angry, brokenhearted ladies in the dating pool who need to be made whole, most often by the next man to come along. (I also suggest the sowing of wild oats, living out your fantasies, and going whatever your version of buck wild is before your commit to a marriage. It's a serious thing that you don't want to take lightly.)

Marriage is about being willing to compromise. When you have a difference of opinion, it's not about being right or wrong, it's about being heard. Understand what your priorities are and look for them in your potential mate. A successful marriage is an ongoing, ever-evolving journey, a labor of love that is built on a solid foundation. Love is *not* enough to make it

all work. Some questions you should ask before making
this type of a commitment:

1. Do you accept each other as you are now?

2. Do you feel you have a solid and enduring
   friendship?

3. Do you have compatible interests, attitudes, values, and goals?

4. Are you willing to accept responsibility for your
   share (an even 50 percent) of making the relationship work?

5. Are you man enough to understand it isn't
   always going to be easy?

The main thing to remember is that you are not missing out on anything. Being able to make love to and build
a life with your best friend is a pretty great deal.

AND NOW FOR THE LADIES!

My wife has done a great job of keeping you on the right path, so I'm going to keep it simple for you. If you're trying early on to figure out a man's intentions with you, the one rule of thumb to keep in mind is, look closely at his actions—they will say it all!

FIVE SIGNS HE'S NOT READY FOR A REAL RELATIONSHIP

1. **He'll tell you!** It may sound harsh, but it's true and fair. If he says he's keeping it loose, you should believe him. Don't think you can do anything to him or for him to change his mind.

2. He's clear about when he wants "relations," but he acts confused when it comes to wanting a relationship. Ever notice how guys never have trouble telling you when they want to have sex? If they can't tell you what they want from your relationship, then they don't want it yet.

3. He shies away from talking about his holiday plans. If spending time with you isn't on the top of his Christmas list, or he isn't sure yet what he's doing for New Year's Eve, you might not want to bank on his sticking around.

4. He hasn't invited you to hang out with his friends and family. Everyone knows these folks are the toughest (and most important) people to please in your companion's life. If after a reasonable time you still haven't spent quality time with his buddies or his kin, you have plenty of progress to make before you can call this a serious relationship.

5. He never calls to take you out, but always suggests staying in. We all know what a guy wants to do when he asks you to stay in—it ain't about saving money and it ain't about making you dinner either.

Once you find a guy whom you want to talk it out with, here's how you'll know he wants the same thing.

FIVE SIGNS THAT YOU'RE HIS GIRL

1. He tells you! (Yeah, that one again.) Guys may not be the clearest communicators, but we know what a serious matter it is to tell a woman she's our one and only. If he tells you that, chances are he means it.

2. He's consistent. Once he stops questioning himself and your relationship, his days of running hot one day and cold the next should be over. Consistency is key.

3. He is considerate of your time and your feelings. You don't have to remind him of your schedule so much anymore—he's aware of your routine and respectful of it.

4. He replaces *I* with *we*. Guys don't do this lightly. When you hear it, you'll know.

5. He stops telling his friends intimate things about you during guy talk. The more he cares about you, the more protective he will become.

I am a happily married man! Lucky for me, my wife lives by the "stomach full, penis empty" rule of thumb—and I am living proof that it works. It's a simple motto with a profound impact on our marriage. I feel spoiled and taken care of, and in exchange I will give her anything or do whatever she asks. We take care of each other. She makes me feel like a king—did she mention that she kisses my feet? And I kiss her *everything*, because she is my queen!

MY HONEY-DO LIST

It didn't take me long to figure out what Niecy likes—ear candy and chores! I learned real quick that if I wanted more action in bed, it would help to put in some work outside of it. In the spirit of honesty, I asked her to tell me some of the things that would turn her on most. She didn't have any trouble coming up with twenty tasks right on the spot. Ladies, feel free to pass this along to your men. And fellas, borrow liberally from this list when you need some extra love leverage.

1. Wash the dishes.

2. Put the toilet seat down.

3. Cook a meal she's never had.

4. Clean her car.

5. Get naked when she least expects it (within reason!).

6. Wash anything you want her to put in her mouth.

7. Wear clean underwear and socks.

8. Buy her favorite flowers—you better learn which kind she likes best!

9. Stop texting other people when you're together.

10. Stop inviting friends along when you go out.

11. Check your breath on the way home from work so she can taste that you were thinking about seeing her.

12. Don't be too hairy.

13. Take an interest in her kids.

14. Take out the trash.

15. Clean up behind yourself and your friends.

16. Get her her own soda at the movies.

17. Use the vacuum.

18. Treat her mother with attentive kindness.

19. Know when to shut up and stop talking.

20. Tell her you love her one more time than you did the day before.

And if anything on this list doesn't feel quite right for you, feel free to improvise! It's all about listening to what makes your partner feel loved and appreciated. Once you have that figured out, deploy as needed!

acknowledgments

I have to thank God for allowing me to experience the heartbreak and heartaches of love while maintaining a spirit so resilient I reached for it again and again.

To the women who have consistently cried, prayed, and celebrated with me while I navigated the many highs and lows of relationships—Dominee Apple, Jamil Barrie, Sharita Yazid, Katie Mae Smith, Sherri Shepherd (the only woman who loves LOVE more than I do), Jill Scott, and my mom, Margaret Ensley—thank you from the bottom of my heart. My journey is still unfolding, so stand by!

Bill Keith, you are my brother from another mother. From our first conversation I felt like you got me . . . now I feel like you are me! Matters of the heart are universal and I thank you for guiding me through it all and sharing your own mayhem and foolishness in the process.

Sending love to my editor Tricia Boczkowski. Sometimes I felt like I was writing this book specifically for you! The book aside, a sisterhood and commonality was present at our first meeting. I didn't know if you would want to work with me after I made you cry! I didn't know exactly the road you traveled down but I could see the end result in your eyes and knew I was on the right track with this book. Thank you for having faith in me and helping me find the funny in what can sometimes be devastating.

I'm also grateful for my Simon & Schuster/Gallery Books family, especially Alexandra Lewis, Jennifer Bergstrom, Louise Burke, and Kristin Dwyer. It takes a village to raise a new writer, and I appreciate your availability to me and this book more than you know.

I'm grateful for my WME family, especially Andy McNichol and Nancy Josephson. Thank you for bringing your client's dreams to fruition.

To my manager, Brian Dobbins—we finally did it! Thank you for always having my back, Dub; I don't take it for granted . . . and I'm glad you always receive the personal love advice I have for you!

Finally, I acknowledge every heartbreak and heartache that led me to the full realization of who I am and what I want. It has all led me to the best thing yet—being my best self for my new husband, Jay.

xoxo,

Niecy Nash Tucker

0546635555